To Lanty, Thanks for your kind and support, best. Now you'll have more time to enjoy. Bon appetit!

Love, Susan Schiff

W9-AZD-743

MAKING IT: IN LESS THAN AN HOUR

A guide to easy gourmet meals

by

Susan Berwind Schiffer

Foods On The Cover

Beverages

MAKING IT in less than an hour

by Susan Berwind Schiffer

Schiffer Publishing Ltd.
EXTON, PENNSYLVANIA

The book is designed by Nancy Schiffer.

The photograph on the cover is by
        Cashen/Stout
        Washington, D.C.

The drawings are by Susie Saunders.

First Edition

Copyright c 1976 by Schiffer Publishing Limited,
Box E, Exton, Pa. 19341

*This book is fully protected by copyright, and, with the
exception of brief excerpts for review, no part of it may be
reprinted in any form by print, photoprint, microfilm or
by any other means without written permission from
the publisher.*

ISBN 0-916838-03-X

Library of Congress Catalog Card Number 76-13410

Printed in the United States of America

1 3 5 6 4 2

This book is dedicated with love to my family without whom neither this book nor anything else would have been possible.

SUSAN B. SCHIFFER

I acknowledge with great gratitude the contributions of the following friends who are expert cooks as well:

Ethel Allen
Nancy Brinker
Irene Cole
Joy Connolly
Patsy Ernst
Tony Ford
Susan Firestone
Rhoulac Hamilton
Beverly Hata
Clark Hooper
Virginia Knauer
Betsy Kleeblatt
Betty Ladd
Peggy McClure
Rosemary O'Neil
Margaret Nutt
Emily Rice
Ginny Sapienza
Mrs. Stewart Saunders, Sr.
Susie Saunders
Maudie Scott
Nina Stanley
Susan Treadway
Watergate Wine and Beverage
Gretchen Wintersteen

TABLE OF CONTENTS

MAKING IT IN LESS THAN AN HOUR means using as few ingredients as possible and simplicity in preparation. To save time, use frozen onions, vegetables and fruits. Dried onion soup is also a useful ingredient. Garlic powder can always be substituted for fresh garlic, margarine for butter, dried herbs for fresh, cool whip for whipped cream, etc.

ABBREVIATIONS

t	=	teaspoon	gal.	=	gallon
T	=	tablespoon	sm.	=	small
oz.	=	ounce	lg.	=	large
C	=	cup	doz.	=	dozen
pt.	=	pint	pkg.	=	package
qt.	=	quart	cond.	=	condensed
lb.	=	pound			

INTRODUCTION

If you neither like to dirty every pan in the kitchen nor have the time to do so, yet like to serve exciting and delicious gourmet meals, this is the cookbook for you. No matter in what fashion you entertain -- be it with a family gathering, cocktail party or all-out crowd scene -- here are dishes to satisfy the most discerning palate, which are economical, dramatic and quick. It is usually possible to prepare all the ingredients required beforehand and quickly cook the food at the last moment.

Making It In Less Than One Hour seeks to bring variety and excitement into your meals and parties even though you have a demanding job or don't have the time or energy to cook all day. This is a true cook's tour, with every recipe you'll need for entertaining with limited time: appetizers and canapes, some hot, others cold; exotic soups with an international flavor; festive meats and vegetables; salads; desserts with the light touch; party drinks -- they're all here, and all yours for the making.

Fully aware as I am that entertaining makes many demands on valuable time, I've made simplicity one of the watchwords throughout the book. Modern "convenience" products go into the recipes wherever they can create maximum good taste (with minimum fuss) and help keep the cook from spending long hours at the stove. To help you enjoy all the gaiety that's going on around you, a goodly portion of the recipes may in some way be prepared in advance.

I've touched each of my recipes with imagination for each basic style of entertaining, from the easy informality of a barbecue or open house or brunch, to the precise elegance of a formal, sit-down dinner; and you'll be pleased, I feel, to combine your favorite ideas with mine. Perhaps you'll come across some new recipes to add to your own menu planning. And so, without further ado, permit me to serve up the gayest, most carefree, most delicious meals ever.

APPETIZER & HORS D'OEUVRE

MUSHROOM AND SNAILS

48 Snails (either with or without shells. Without is easier.)
24 Medium Mushrooms (fresh is better; canned is okay.)
½ C Minced Shallots
2 T Minced Celery
1 T Minced Garlic
4 Sticks (2 C) Butter
¼ C Minced Parsley
  Lemon Juice, Salt, Pepper, to taste

To make the galic butter, saute ¼ C shallots in 1 T butter until they are softened.

Stir in the celery and garlic and remove the pan from the heat.

In a bowl combine butter, softened, and shallot mixture, and add other ingredients.

If using shells, put about 1 t of garlic butter in each shell.

Put snails in recesses of dishes, adding any extra butter around them and on top of mushrooms.

Put in preheated 450° oven for 10 minutes or until the butter is bubbly.

Make sure during cooking that butter is melting on the mushrooms also by stirring.

Serve with French Bread.

Serves eight.

CRABMEAT STUFFED ARTICHOKES

2   Small Cans of Crabmeat
1   Stick of Butter
    Salt and Pepper, to taste
1   Can Cream of Mushroom Soup
2   T Parmesan Cheese
8   Artichoke Bottoms

Saute the crabmeat in butter.

Add salt and pepper.

Combine mixture with soup and cheese, and place in artichoke bottoms.

Place artichokes under broiler until they are brown, then serve.

Serves four.

EASY OYSTERS ROCKEFELLER

Oysters on the Half Shell (allow 6 Oysters per person)
1 T Cooked Spinach, Chopped
1 T Hollandaise Sauce
Dash of Nutmeg
Gruyere Cheese, to Taste
Bacon Bits, to Taste

Place on each shell:
1 T cooked, chopped spinach. Add dash of nutmeg on top.

Place on top of oyster next:
1 T Hollandaise Sauce which has been mixed with Gruyere Cheese and Bacon Bits, to taste.

Freeze or refrigerate.

Bake at 450° to 500° for 10 minutes or until oysters are plump and brown, and then put under broiler for the last minute or two.

MUSHROOM AND ARTICHOKE APPETIZER

2 Small Jars of Mushrooms in Vinegrette
2 Small Jars of Marinated Artichokes
1 t Tarragon
1 t Chives
1 t Thyme

Drain artichokes.

Mix artichokes with mushrooms (with their vinegar) and herb s

This salad can be left in refrigerator for use when people drop by.

If serving as a first course, place salad on lettuce leaf.

Serves four.

MUSHROOMS STUFFED WITH CRAB

36 Mushroom Caps, washed
2 lbs. Crab Meat
2 Sticks Butter
   Lemon, to Taste
   White Wine, to Taste or ½ C
   Dash of Paprika
   Parsley
   Salt and Pepper, to Taste

Cut and wash mushrooms.

Meanwhile, saute crab meat (canned is OK) using butter with about ½ C white wine, salt, pepper and lemon juice.

Stuff mushrooms with mixture.

Add paprika and parsley on top.

Bake in preheated oven at 400⁰ for 8 minutes.

BRAISED ENDIVE AND BACON

2 Endives
2 Strips of Bacon
  Salt and Pepper, to Taste

Trim endive and peel off outer leaves.

Wrap bacon around endive and place in a small casserole.

Add salt and pepper and cook covered until the endive is tender.

Serves two.

POTTED SHRIMP

3 Jars Tiny Danish Shrimp
½ Stick Butter
  Cayenne Pepper, to Taste
  Garlic Powder, to Taste (optional)

Drain shrimp and pack firmly into a serving dish or individual casserole.

Heat butter in saucepan, adding herbs and pour over shrimp just enough to cover shrimp.

Chill.

Serve with toast.

PROSCIUTTO AND CRABMEAT

3 Slices Prosciutto per serving
¼ C crabmeat
3 T Butter
  Lemon Wedges

Roll up crabmeat in 3 slices of prosciutto.

Brown in butter.

Serve with lemon wedges.

BOURSIN MUSHROOMS

Mushroom Caps, Washed
Boursin Cheese
Paprika

Stuff raw, washed mushroom caps with Boursin Cheese.

Sprinkle paprika on top and serve.

Mushrooms can also be filled with sour cream and horseradish to taste — or bought processed spreads.

BACON CRISPS

Bacon Slices
Ritz Crackers
Chutney (optional)

Wrap ½ slice of bacon around each Ritz Cracker.

Place crackers on aluminum pan and bake for 15 minutes or until bacon is done.

Every 5 minutes turn the crackers, so the bacon cooks completely and the crackers absorb the fat.

If you like Chutney, place it on the crackers the last time you turn them.

JOY CONNOLLY'S CAVIAR AND EGG

1 Small Jar of Caviar
6 Hard-Boiled Eggs
½ T Half and Half Cream
1 T Mayonnaise
1 spoonful of Cream

Line the bottom of a small glass bowl with caviar, reserving enough to cover the top.

Finely chop egg yolks and ¾ of egg whites.

Mix eggs with Half and Half and mayonnaise, and evenly spread mixture in dish.

Top eggs with remaining caviar and cream.

Garnish with parsley and surround dish with crackers or melba toast.

(The clear glass dish allows your guests to see the egg mixture.)

EASY PATE

3 Cans Liver Pate (small)
2 Cans Gooseliver Pate
1 Stick Butter
1 T Dijon Mustard
1 Pkg. Onion Soup Mix
1 t Port
1 t Brandy

Saute all ingredients together in butter.

Chill and serve. Can be stored in ice box for weeks.

(Very good in raw mushrooms)

SEAFOOD MOUSSE

1 Can Cream of Tomato Soup
1 Can Water (using soup can as measuring instrument)
2 T Lemon Juice
¼ C Onion, finely chopped
1 T Parsley Flakes
1 T Celery Leaves
1 t Basil
1 (8 oz.) Pkg. Cream Cheese
½ C Mayonnaise
1 Pkg. Plain Gelatin
2 T Water
2 or 3 C Cooked Shrimp and Crabmeat, chopped

Prepare soup with water and add seasonings. Simmer for 5 minutes, removing celery leaves.

Remove from heat and beat in cream cheese which has been cubed. Add mayonnaise.

Return to heat and add gelatin which has been softened in 2 T water and stir well.

Cool and fold in seafood. Check seasoning and pour into fish-shaped mold and refrigerate until firm.

Unmold on chopped greens and decorate with shrimp, olives, green pepper strips or other garnish.

Serve with melba toast as a spread.

(May also be served as a molded gelatin salad with the addition of chopped celery and green pepper.)

PARMESAN TOAST

¼ lb. Butter, softened
¾ C Parmesan Cheese, grated
½ t Tabasco Sauce
1 Pkg. Melba Toast or Garlic Rounds

Place butter in mixing bowl. Add cheese and Tabasco Sauce and mix well.

Spread mixture on toasts and put under broiler for 2 to 3 minutes until cheese bubbles.

Makes approximately 20.

PEANUT SURPRISES

1/2 C Peanut Butter (chunky is best)
1/3 C Chutney
1/4 C Bacon Bits (optional)

Mix all ingredients well and spread on crackers.

Place on baking sheet and put under broiler until brown and melted.

Depending on cracker size, makes 12 to 20.

(Mixture can be stored in refrigerator and used whenever guests drop by)

NEW POTATOES

New Potatoes
Sour Cream
Chives or Caviar
Salt and Pepper, to Taste

Cook new potatoes until tender.

Scoop out a cavity.

Combine sour cream, chives or caviar and seasonings to taste.

THE MYSTERY MAN'S CUCUMBER AND CAVIAR CANAPES

(I cannot tell you who gave me this recipe because he modestly declined to take the credit for something he is not sure whether he was the first to think of it, but I think they are both super.)

2 Large Skinned Cucumbers
½ Pt. Sour Cream
1 Jar Caviar
1 Lemon

Slice the cucumbers and place a dollop of sour cream on top.

Spoon some caviar on each piece.

Squeeze a bit of lemon juice on top of each and refrigerate for 30 minutes.

Makes approximately 20 canapes.

(At Christmas time, it is festive to use red caviar.)

CHERRY TOMATOES DIPPED IN VODKA

Cherry Tomatoes
Vodka
Jane's Krazy Salt

Wash and de-stem tomatoes.

Marinate in vodka for several hours and then roll in salt.

EASY PICKLED MUSHROOMS

1   C White Wine Vinegar
½   C Water
2   T Sugar
1½ C Salt
1   T Minced Garlic
2   Small Bay Leaves
6   Cloves
1   lb. Canned Button Mushrooms, drained

Combine in sauce pan the first seven ingredients and heat until well mixed.

Add mushrooms and place in refrigerator.

After several days, mushrooms can be eaten and they will last for months.

(Cocktail onions can also be added for a good variation.)

STUFFED MUSHROOMS PARMESAN

1   Stick of Butter
1   C Onions, chopped (frozen is fine)
1/3 C Parmesan Cheese, grated
2   C Progresso Italian Bread Crumbs
1   t Paprika
24 Large Mushrooms, washed and stems removed

Saute onions in butter.

Add cheese, bread crumbs and paprika.

Stuff mushrooms and place on flat pan and bake at 350° for 25 minutes.

CURRIED CASHEWS

2 C Cashew Nuts
2 T Butter
1 t   Salt
1 T Curry Powder

Saute nuts in butter until brown.

Drain.

Combine nuts with salt and curry powder.

Serve hot or cold with cocktails.

SPICED CASHEWS

Substitute ½ t Cayenne and ½ t Cumin for curry powder.

SIMPLE THINGS TO SERVE WITH COCKTAILS

HOT SALAMI

Broil slices of salami in a hot oven for a few minutes until crisp.

Serve warm.

COLD SALAMI AND ONIONS

Combine slices of salami and cocktail onions on a toothpick and serve.

HOT WALNUTS

Put 1 cup walnut meats in an oiled baking dish and bake for 10 to 12 minutes at 350°.

Spread on a large sheet of waxed paper.

Sprinkle with 1 tsp. salt, 1 tsp. curry powder and a dash of paprika.

Gather up ends of waxed paper and shake well until nuts are well coated with seasonings.

Serve warm.

SOUR CREAM DIP OR SAUCE

1 (8 oz.) carton Sour Cream
2 T Horseradish
½ T Paprika

Combine all ingredients, blending well and serve with chips and/or vegetables as a dip and as a sauce for roast beef.

GINNY'S WINTER SURPRISES

Leftover or Canned Corned Beef Hash
Chutney (1/3 chutney to 2/3 hash)
Toast Rounds or Crackers

Combine hash and chutney and spread on crackers.

Place under the broiler until browned.

GINNY'S SUMMER SURPRISE

2 Cans Avocado Mix or Guacamole Mix
½ Pt. Sour Cream
1 Box of Cherry Tomatoes or 4 large Cucumbers
1 Loaf of Bread, thinly sliced or 1 box of Cocktail Bread Rounds

If you are using fresh bread, with a 50 cent size cutter, cut bread and toast until they are stiff.

Mix the avocado and sour cream.

Slice tomatoes very thinly.

Place a tomato slice on each bread round, and then add avocado mixture using a pastry tube or butter knife to spread it.

Makes approximately 50 hors d'oeuvres.

NINA'S SINFUL DELIGHTS

1 Can of Crabmeat
2 T Mayonnaise
½ t Curry Powder
1 T Grated Romano or Parmesan Cheese
   Salt and Pepper, to taste
1 Sm. Pkg. Cream Cheese, softened
1 Pkg. Toast Rounds or cocktail Croutelletes (pastry shells)

Combine and mash the first six ingredients until the mixture is of spreadable consistency, and place in refrigerator for 30 minutes until mixture is slightly harder.

Spread mixture generously on toast rounds or into pastry shells and place under broiler until browned.

RAREBIT CANAPES

1   Stick Butter, softened
1   C Sharp Cheddar or Parmesan Cheese, grated
½   t Pepper
½   t Powdered Mustard
1   t Parsley Flakes
½   C Dry Sherry
24 Melba Toasts or Garlic Rounds

Combine all ingredients well and spread on toast.

Place under broiler for 1 to 2 minutes or until cheese turns brown.

Makes 24 canapes.

COCKTAIL BEETS

2 Jars Cooked Whole Beets
1 Container Sour Cream
   Horseradish, to Taste

Combine sour cream and horseradish and put into a serving bowl on a tray.

Put toothpicks in beets and place on tray for dipping.

CHIPPED BEEF DIP

2 T Heavy Cream
1 8 oz. Pkg. Cream Cheese
1 8 oz. Pkg. Chopped Chipped Beef
1 T Horseradish
1 Medium Onion, Finely Chopped
   Dash of Worcestershire Sauce
   Rye Crackers

Soften cheese with cream.

Add onion, horseradish and Worcestershire Sauce and mix well.

Shape into ball and wrap chipped beef around cheese and chill.

Serve with rye crackers.

CLAM CANAPES

1 Pkg. Cream Cheese
1 Can Minced Clams, Drained
   Salt, to Taste
   Dash of Red Pepper
3 t Worcestershire Sauce
1 t Minced Green Onion
   Melba Toast or Other Plain Cracker

Whip the cream cheese with a fork.

Add clams and mix well.

Add remaining ingredients and whip well.

Place in ice box in covered container.

When ready to cook, heap generously on melba toast or other plain cracker and bake at 300° for 20 minutes.

Sprinkle with paprika for looks.

BLENDER CREAM CHEESE SPREADS

Cream Cheese
Watercress, washed

Blend cream cheese and watercress. Spread on toast or bread rounds.

Cream cheese
Cucumber, washed
Onion, peeled

Blend cream cheese, cucumber and onion. Spread on toast or bread rounds.

Cream cheese
Horseradish
Cooked Beef Slices

Blend cream cheese and horseradish to taste. Stuff beef slices with mixture.

Cream cheese
Chipped Beef
Sweet Pickles

Blend cream cheese, chipped beef and pickles. Spread on toast or bread rounds.

CAVIAR HORS D'OEUVRES

1½ (8 oz.) Pkgs. Cream Cheese
1   Envelope Lipton Onion Soup Mix
1   Box Cocktail Pastry Shells
2   (2 oz.) Jars of Caviar

Mix softened cream cheese with onion soup mix.

Put mixture into pastry shells and spread caviar on top.

HAM CANAPES

1 C Deviled Ham Mix
2 t Minced Onion
½ t Powdered Mustard
1 t Black Pepper
½ Stick Butter
¼ C Sour Cream
1 Can Refrigerator Biscuits

Mix first six ingredients and place in the middle of biscuit dough.

Bake the biscuits according to directions.

MUSHROOM CANAPES

½ lb. Mushrooms, Washed and Chopped
2½ Sticks Butter, Softened
¼ t Black Pepper
¼ t Salt
3 T Dry Sherry or Brandy

Saute mushrooms in one stick of butter for 8 to 10 minutes.

Put mushrooms and other ingredients in blender and blend until smooth.

Serve on crackers, toast or in cocktail pastry shells.

Parsley or Fines Herbs can be added.

BLEU CHEESE BALL

1 Lg. Pkg. Cream Cheese, softened
Bleu Cheese, to Taste
Dried Mint and Onion Flakes

Combine cream cheese and bleu cheese mixing well.

Roll cheese into a ball and then roll in mint and onion flakes.

CURRY DIP

```
 1    C Mayonnaise
1½    T Mustard Pickle Relish
1-1/3 T Curry Powder
1-1/3 T Dijon Mustard
      Potato Chips or Raw Vegetables
```

Combine all ingredients well.

Serve with potato chips or raw vegetables.

RED CAVIAR DIP

```
¼ C Cream Cheese
1  C Sour Cream
2  T Grated Onion
1½ lb. Red Caviar (2 small jars)
```

Combine cream cheese, sour cream and onion and whip well.

Fold in caviar gently and chill.

HORSERADISH CREAM CHEESE DIP

2 (3 oz.) Pkgs. Cream Cheese
¼ C Sour Cream
2 to 4 T Freshly Grated Horseradish
    Salt and Pepper, to Taste
    Paprika, to Taste
    Tabasco Sauce, to Taste
2 T Chopped Parsley

Mash cream cheese and gradually blend in sour cream.

Add horseradish and seasonings and beat until mixture is light and fluffy.

Chill.

Serve with a sprinkle of parsley and raw vegetables cut into bite-size pieces.

CHILLED SPINACH DIP

1 Pkg. Frozen Chopped Spinach
    Juice of 2 Lemons
¼ lb. Roquefort Cheese
¼ C Sour Cream

Prepare spinach according to directions.

Add lemon juice and roquefort cheese to sour cream and mix well.

Add to spinach and chill.

Serve well chilled with chips or vegetables.

ARTICHOKES WITH OYSTER DIP

2 Lg. Artichokes, cooked and chilled (or one can of artichokes)
16 Frozen Oysters, thawed and drained
¼ t Tabasco Sauce
2 Scallions, white part only
1 T Lemon Juice
½ t Salt
1 Pt. Sour Cream
Dash of Paprika

Remove artichoke leaves placing them around the edge of a serving plate.

Dice artichoke hearts coarsely and put in a blender.

Add oysters, tabasco sauce, scallion, lemon juice and salt and blend at high speed for 10 seconds or until smooth.

Mix in well the sour cream.

Pour into a serving bowl and dust with paprika.

Chill until serving time.

GOURMET CHEESE BALL

3 (8 oz.) Pkgs. Cream Cheese, softened
2 Jars Chutney, drained
1 (5 oz.) Can Dried Roasted Buttered Almonds
Curry Powder, to Taste
3 T Butter

Brown almonds in butter.

Shape cream cheese into a ball.

Place chutney on cheese ball and add almonds.

GUACAMOLE

3 Soft Ripe Avocadoes
1 C Green Onion, thinly cut
2 T Lime Juice
¼ t Tabasco Sauce
1 t Salt
  Garlic Powder, to Taste
  Tomato Paste, to Taste
  Melba Toast or Corn Chips

Place all ingredients in blender and blend until smooth.

Serve with melba toast or corn chips.

DEVILED HAM DIP

2 (4½ oz.) Cans Deviled Ham
1 (8 oz.) Pkg. Cream Cheese
1 T Catsup
2 T Finely Chopped Onion
3 T Chopped Stuffed Green Olives

Combine all ingredients and mix well and refrigerate to chill.

Makes two cups.

EGG SALAD HORS' D'OEUVRES

1 Quart bought egg salad (or homemade with extra onions, celery, freshly ground black pepper, and a dash of horse-radish)
1 pint Sour Cream
3-4 jars Caviar

Mold the egg salad on a platter or serving dish. Ice with sour cream as you would a cake. Spoon the caviar on top of the mold. Serve with slices of party pumpernickel and/or rye.

Serves 24-30 at a cocktail party (depending on whatever else you are serving).

MINIATURE PIZZAS

2 boxes of tiny Pastry Shells (coquilletes) or melba rounds
1 large jar of Ragu Spaghetti Sauce
½T Garlic Powder
½T Oregano
½T Italian Herbs
1 C Bacon bits, chunks of Pepperoni or Salami
8 ounces of Mozzarella or Parmesan Cheese

Mix all ingredients except the cheese. Place in the shells or on the rounds. Sprinkle with cheese. Bake five minutes or until the cheese melts. Serve hot.

Makes about fifty miniature pizzas.

HOT DOG APPETIZERS

½C Soy Sauce
1 T Sugar
1 T Minced Onion
1 t Ginger
¼C Bourbon (optional)
1 package of Hot Dogs

Cut the hot dogs into bite size pieces and marinate in the mixture for several hours. Place the hot dogs and sauce in a shallow baking dish and bake at 350º for about fifteen minutes or until thoroughly heated. Drain and serve with tooth picks.

SWEDISH MEATBALLS

1½ lbs. Ground Beef
4   Medium Onions, chopped
6   T Butter
1   Egg
 ½t Nutmeg
1   t Paprika
1½t Salt
1   C Zwieback or Cracker Crumbs
6   T Milk

Saute onions in butter until browned.

Beat egg in a large bowl and add all ingredients, mixing well.

Form meat into small balls and brown on all sides; cover and simmer 5 minutes.

Add just enough flour, water and beef bouillon cubes to make a gravy.

Cook slowly for 15 minutes.

Six servings of about eighteen 1½ inch meat balls.

ARTICHOKE HORS D'OEUVRES

Marinated Artichokes
Bacon strips
Toothpicks

Slice each artichoke heart in half.

Slice bacon strips in half and cook just slightly.

Wrap bacon around artichoke, fasten with toothpick and place under broiler for a few minutes until bacon is cooked.

SOUPS

EASY GASPACHO

1 Bottle of Bloody Mary Mix
1 T Olive Oil
2 T Minced Garlic or Garlic Powder
1 Green Pepper, Seeded and Chopped
1 Cucumber, Peeled and Dried
2 Peeled, Seeded Tomatoes
½t Salt
½t Black Pepper
1 T Grated Onion

Put 1 C of Bloody Mary Mix in blender with half of the vegetables and add other ingredients.

If you like thicker Gaspacho, add extra cucumber and tomato.

Serve with croutons and diced vegetables: green peppers, celery, cucumbers, onions and tomatoes.

Easy croutons can be made by sauteing seasoned croutons in butter with garlic salt to taste. Make the croutons at the last minute.

Serves six.

EASY ONION SOUP

2 Cans Onion Soup
2 T Calvados or Apple Brandy
2 Pats of Butter
  Black Pepper, to Taste
  Slices of Buttered Melba Toast
  Parmesan Cheese, to garnish

Mix first four ingredients and pour into individual pots.

Place melba toast on top, adding parmesan cheese and place under broiler until browned.

Serves seven.

BOULLA BOULLA SOUP

1 Can Pea Soup
1 Can Beef Boullion
1 Can Tomato Soup
1 C Sherry
  Pepper, to Taste
1 Can Canned Crabmeat or large dollop of Sour Cream

Combine all ingredients in large pan, adding pepper to taste.

Add crabmeat or sour cream and serve.

Serves six.

EASY CURRY SOUP

1 Pkg. Frozen Vegetable (peas, spinach or broccoli)
3 Cans Vichyssoise Soup
  Curry Powder, to Taste

Place thawed vegetable and 2 cans of soup in a blender and puree until smooth.

Add curry powder and other can of soup.

Chill and serve.

Serves six.

ICED AVOCADO SOUP

1 Can (10½ oz.) Chicken Consomme
3 Ripe Avocadoes
½ C Light Cream
1 Finely Chopped Silver Onion
1 t each Salt and Pepper
3 T Worcestershire Sauce
2 C Milk

Combine ingredients and blend well.

Serve chilled.

Serves 6.

VEGETABLE AND APRICOT SOUP

24 ounces of mixed vegetables, frozen or canned
1 package of dried Apricots
1 package of frozen Onions
1 stick of Butter
1 pint of Chicken or Beef Stock
1 C White Wine (with chicken stock) or Red Wine (with beef stock)
1 T Parsley
1 T Fines Herbs
   Salt and Pepper to Taste

Saute the onions in butter until golden. Add all other ingredients, cover, and simmer for an hour, stirring occasionally.

Serves eight.

EASY SPINACH SOUP

1 Pkg. Frozen Spinach
1 Can Mushroom Soup
1 Stick Butter
   Salt and Pepper, to Taste
1 Can Milk (using soup can as measuring can) or ½ milk and ½ white wine

Cook spinach and soup separately according to directions.

Add butter, salt and pepper.

Add spinach to soup and serve.

(The spinach can be pureed in the blender, if you prefer.)

Serves four to six.

TOMATO AND CHIVE SOUP

2 C Canned Tomatoes
2 T Diced Onion (frozen may be used)
1 Stalk of Celery, chopped
2 Pts. Sour Cream
  Chopped Chives, to garnish

On the day before serving, boil the first three ingredients, strain and chill.

Before serving mix soup with equal parts of sour cream, sprinkle chives on top and serve — very cold.

Serves seven.

EASY CURRIED SOUP

1 Can Golden Mushroom Soup
1 Can Cream of Celery Soup
1 Can Water (using soup can as a measuring instrument)
1 Can Chicken in Broth
2 T Butter
2 T Curry Powder
  Salt and Pepper, to Taste

Combine all ingredients in a large saucepan.

Heat and serve.

Serves six.

EASY CLAM CHOWDER

2 Cans of Clam Chowder (Snow's is very good.)
½ Can of Milk, using soup can as measuring instrument
1 Stick of Butter
1 C Onions, sliced (frozen may be used)
1 t Lemon Pepper
1 t Jane's Krazy Salt
1 Can Clams with broth
   Bacon Bits or Oyster Crackers

In a soup pan, saute clams and onions in butter.

Add remaining ingredients and simmer until hot.

Serve with bacon bits or oyster crackers.

Serves four to six.

PEANUT SOUP

2 T Butter
1 T Onion, minced
5 T Chunky Peanut Butter
2 T Flour
2 C Milk, heated
1 C Chicken Stock
Salt and Pepper, to Taste
Chopped Peanuts, to garnish

Saute onions in butter and add peanut butter.

Add flour and stir.

Add milk and chicken stock, stirring until blended and adding salt and pepper.

Pour into a double boiler and simmer for 20 minutes.

Garnish with peanuts and serve. Serves four.

CREAM OF ONION AND CELERY SOUP

1 Can Cream of Celery Soup
1 C Onions, sliced
1 Stick Butter
Salt, Pepper and Garlic Powder, to Taste
2 Cans Milk
½t Fines Herbs
½t Ground Nutmeg
1 T Parsley Flakes

Heat soup and milk in large pot.

Saute onions in butter and add to soup.

Ad herbs and season to taste.

Serves four.

EASY OYSTER STEW

1 Can Cream of Celery Soup
1 Can Cream of Potato Soup or Vichyssoise
1 Pt. of Oysters
½ Stick of Butter
   Salt and Pepper, to Taste
   Sherry, to Taste

Heat soups until boiling point.

Add oysters, butter and seasonings and bring to a boil.

Add sherry and serve.

Serves four.

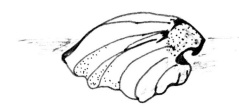

EASY CRAB SOUP

2 Cans Cream of Celery Soup
1½ Can of Milk (using soup can as a measuring instrument)
½ Can of Sherry (using soup can as a measuring instrument)
1 lb. Crabmeat
   Salt and Pepper, to Taste
   Pinch of Fine Herbs

Combine all ingredients in a saucepan and heat.

Serves six.

CAULIFLOWER AND ONION SOUP

1 C Onion, Chopped
1 Stick Butter
2 T Flour
2½ C Chicken Broth
2 C Cauliflower Florets
1 C Cream
    Cayenne, Salt and Pepper, to Taste
    Fines Herbs may also be added, to Taste

In large saucepan saute onions in butter and then add flour.

Remove pan from heat, add broth and cauliflower, and stir and bring the liquid to a boil. Simmer for 30 minutes or until cauliflower is very tender.

Puree the mixture in a blender in two batches and return it to saucepan.

Add cream and seasonings to taste.

Before serving, cook the soup until heated. Pour into bowls and sprinkle parsley on top.

Serves Four.

COLD ASPARAGUS SOUP

1 lb. Frozen Asparagus or ½ lb. fresh
4 T Butter
½ C Thinly Sliced Onions
3 C Chicken Stock
2 T Flour
2 t Lemon Juice
4 t Celery Salt
   Salt and Pepper, to Taste
1½ C Heavy Cream

Cut off tips from 6 asparagus stalks and reserve for garnish. Cut rest of asparagus into 1" pieces and put into a flat pan.

Add butter, onions and ½ cup chicken stock; cover and simmer until asparagus is tender (about 7 minutes for frozen or 12 minutes for fresh).

Using a strainer, remove asparagus from pan and put into a blender.

Meanwhile, poach the tips in boiling salt water until tender, drain and refrigerate.

Add flour to ¼ cup chicken stock to make paste in pan. Add rest of stock, lemon juice, celery salt, salt and pepper; simmer for 10 minutes.

Add stock to asparagus in blender and puree.

Return to pan and simmer another 5 minutes. Taste and adjust seasoning and refrigerate.

To Serve: Spoon cold soup into individual cups and garnish with an asparagus tip.

Serves eight.

ZUCCHINI SOUP

1 Stick Butter
1 lb. Zucchini Squash, Washed and sliced into thin rounds
1 T Garlic Powder
½ to 1 t Curry Powder
1 t Italian Herbs
   Salt and Pepper, to Taste
¼ C Chopped Onions
1 Can Chicken Broth
½ C Heavy Cream

Saute zucchini in butter with herbs until it is limp.

Place all ingredients in blender and blend until well mixed.

Chill and serve with sprigs of parsley.

Serves seven.

ZUCCHINI SOUP

3 T Butter
¼ C Oil
1 Medium-Sized Onion, Chopped
4 to 5 Zucchini Squash, Shredded
   Salt and Pepper, to Taste
2 T Flour
1 C Boullion Beef Broth
1 C Water

Using butter and oil, saute onion.

Add Zucchini and saute.

Add other ingredients and simmer for 15 minutes and serve.
Serves four to six.

PINK MUSHROOM SOUP

1 Can Tomato Soup
1 Can Pea Soup
1 Can Cream of Mushroom Soup
1½ Can Milk (using soup can as measuring can)
1½ Can White Wine
    Fresh Mushrooms and Parsley, finely chopped for garnish

Put all soups in large pot and add milk and wine.

Heat and serve with garnish.

Serves six to eight.

CURRIED PEA SOUP — HOT OR COLD

½ lb. Butter
1 C Onions, chopped
3 Cans Pea Soup
2 t Garlic
2 Cans Chicken Stock
1 t Salt
1 t Pepper
½ t Sugar
1 t Cardamon Seed
1 C Heavy Cream
1 C Regular Cream or half and half
2 T Curry Powder

Saute onions in butter in large saucepan.

Add all ingredients, mixing well and simmer until fully blended.

If serving cold, let cool, add 1 cup heavy cream (whipped) and just before serving, add 1 cup light cream and 1 tablespoon curry powder.

If serving hot, add both types of cream at once with curry powder. Serves eight.

SHRIMP BISQUE

1 Can Green Pea Soup
1 Can Tomato Soup
1 Can Whole Milk (using soup can as a measuring instrument)
1 C Water
1 C Sherry
½ lb. Cooked Shrimp, chopped or Danish Shrimp

Combine all ingredients in a large pot and stir well over medium heat.

Heat and serve.

Serves eight.

PEA SOUP LOUISE

1 Can Condensed Cream of Pea Soup
1/2 C Water
1 Chicken Boullion Cube
1/8 t Mace
1/4 t Dried Tarragon
1/2 C Cream
1/2 C Dry White Wine or Champagne
    Fresh mint or Tarragon

Simmer together in large saucepan the soup, water, boullion, mace and tarragon for ½ hour.

Before serving add cream and wine and heat.

Garnish with mint or tarragon.

Serves four.

COLD CUCUMBER AND SPINACH SOUP

1 Bunch Scallions, sliced
4 T Butter
4 C Cucumbers, diced
3 C Chicken Broth
1 C Spinach, chopped
½C Potatoes, sliced (optional)
½t Salt
   Lemon Juice, to Taste
   Pepper, to Taste
¼C Light Cream
   Slices of Cucumber, Radishes and Scallions

In a large saucepan, saute scallions in butter until softened.

Add cucumbers, chicken broth, spinach, potatoes and seasonings.

Simmer until potatoes are tender.

Transfer mixture in batches to a blender and puree it.

Pour puree into a bowl and stir in light cream.

Let soup cool and chill for 2 hours.

Garnish with thin slices of cucumber, radishes and scallions.

Serves eight.

CREAM OF SPINACH SOUP

1 Small Onion, chopped
1 Pkg. Frozen Spinach, cooked
1 Pt. Sour Cream
2 C Chicken Broth

Prepare spinach according to directions.

Place in blender half of onion, spinach, sour cream and chicken broth and puree until smooth.

Repeat for remainder of ingredients.

Serve hot or cold.

Serves four.

EASY CLAM BISQUE

1 Can Tomato Soup
1 Can Pea Soup
1 Can Cream of Mushroom Soup
2½ C Milk or Half & Half
1 (10 oz.) Can of Minced Clams
½ C Sherry

Combine all ingredients, except sherry in a large pot and bring to a boil.

Reduce heat, add sherry and serve.

Serves eight.

CREAM OF PEANUT SOUP GLACE

¼ C Butter
1 Lg. Rib Celery, sliced thin
1 Medium Yellow Onion, minced
½ C Cold Water
2 T Flour
6 (10½ oz.) Cans of Chicken Broth
1 (12 oz.) Jar of Creamy Peanut Butter
1 C Light Cream
    Sour Cream, to garnish
    Chopped Chives, to garnish

Melt butter in a large heavy saucepan.

Add celery, onion and water and bring to a boil over moderate heat until all of the water has evaporated and the vegetables are soft.

Stir in flour and continue to cook, stirring constantly for 4 minutes and then add chicken broth and bring to a boil over high heat.

Add peanut butter, whipping with a wire whisk until mixture is smooth.

Reduce heat and simmer for 15 minutes.

Remove mixture from heat and stir in cream.

Seal with plastic wrap and chill until cold.

Serve in chilled soup bowls with a dollop of sour cream and chopped chives.

Serves eight.

SEAFOOD

GARLIC TAILS

4 Lobster Tails
½ Stick of Butter
½ t Garlic Powder
½ C Chutney

Cut off lobster shell with the exception of the tail (one slice down the back and then across the center is the easiest method).

In a small saucepan, melt butter and garlic, and brush on lobster tails.

Place lobster under broiler for 5 minutes or until both sides are turning light brown.

Serve with small bowls of chutney for dipping.

(Lemon slices can also be added for garnish, but are not needed.)

Serves four.

SESAME SCALLOPS

½ lb. Bacon
2 lbs. Scallops
1 C Sesame Seeds
   Lemon Slices

Cook bacon and wrap around scallops that have been rolled in sesame seeds.

Place scallops on skewers and broil 5 to 10 minutes.

Serve with lemon slices.

Serves four as an appetizer or two for dinner.

STEAK - LOBSTER KEBABS

 1 Bottle Italian Salad Dressing
 1 C Vodka or Gin
 1 T Black Pepper
 1 T Salt
 1 T Fine Herbs
   Juice of 2 Lemons
12 Cherry Tomatoes
12 Chunks of either Fresh or Canned Pineapple
12 Onions, canned kind for roasts
12 Slices of Green Pepper
 3 Lobster Tails, cut into cubes
 3 lbs. Steak or Fondue Meat, cubed

Combine first 6 ingredients in flat dish suitable for marinating.

Slice lobster and steaks and marinate them for 3-4 hours.

When ready to cook, alternate ingredients on skewers.

Cook over outside grill, medium heat, 300° four minutes each side. Under a broiler about the same time, but keep checking to make sure not too well done.

Use extra marinade for juice during cooking if outside, but don't get too close.

Serve six generously.

JOY CONNOLLY'S OVEN POACHED SALMON

2 lbs. Fresh Salmon, boned
  Salt and Pepper, to taste
½C of V-8 Juice to ¾ C Dry White Wine, to use as cooking
  liquid, as needed
  Slices of Lemon, Parsley and Carrots, to garnish

Place salmon on large sheet of heavy duty foil and shape into a tent.

Lightly add salt and pepper to inside of salmon. Add cooking liquid until fish is ¾ covered, and add salt and pepper.

Cook at 325º for approximately 25 minutes per pound.

Arrange salmon on platter with sides spread flat and garnish with slices of lemon, parsley and carrots.

Serves as either a first course or as a main course, especially at a summer party.

A green or plain mayonnaise is good with it.

FILET OF SOLE IN VERMOUTH

3 lbs. Sole Fillets
1 Stick Butter
  Juice of 1 Lemon
2 C Dry Vermouth or White Wine
  Salt and Pepper to Taste

Heat the butter and 1 C vermouth.

Add the sole and saute for about five minutes on each side (sole can be dipped in bread crumbs first).

Add other cup vermouth and dash of parsley just before serving.

Seedless grapes can also be added when cooking.

FISH BAKED IN FOIL

1½ Sticks of Butter
 1 C Onions, chopped
 ½ C Green Peppers, chopped
 2 T Parsley, chopped
 1 t Salt
 1 t Pepper
1½ C Mushrooms, chopped
 2 lbs. Fresh fish or 4 portions of frozen fish
    Flour for dredging

Preheat oven to 375° or start grill fire.

Saute onions in butter until tender and add peppers, parsley, salt and pepper and mushrooms and cook for 3 minutes.

Dredge fish in flour and place each on a large sheet of foil.

Divide vegetables into four servings, placing each portion on top of each portion of fish; wrap fish.

Bake for 25 minutes in the oven or 10 minutes on each side, if using a grill.

Serves four.

EASY DIETETIC BROILED FISH

¼ C Dietetic Italian Dressing
1 t Grated Lemon Peel
¼ C Fresh Lemon Juice
1 t Crazy Jane Salt
1 t Pepper
1 T Parsley
2 T Dijon Mustard
1 Whole Lemon, Quartered
  Parsley Sprigs
1½ lbs. Frozen or Fresh Fish Fillets

Combine first seven ingredients and mix well.

Place fish in shallow pan and pour sauce over fish.

Broil fish 5 to 8 minutes about 7 inches from the flame.

While cooking, brush fish several times with sauce; the fish does not need to be turned.

Serve with parsley sprigs and quartered lemon.

Serves four.

❧ SCALLOPS AND ONIONS

1 Pkg. Bacon
2 lbs. Sea Scallops
2 Cans Onions
  Thyme and Tarragon, to Taste

Saute bacon strips until they are transparent and cut them into thirds.

Sprinkle scallops with thyme and tarragon.

Wrap each scallop with bacon and thread on skewers alternately with onions.

Cook over a hot barbecue or broil them until bacon is crisp and onions are tender.

Serve with tartar sauce or orange-horseradish sauce.

Serves four.

MARINATED SKEWERED SCALLOPS

2 T Lemon Juice
¼ C Salad Oil
½ t Basil
  Ground Pepper
2 lbs. Scallops
½ lb. Bacon

Combine lemon juice, oil, basil and pepper in a bowl.

Place scallops in marinade for 1 hour.

Cook bacon half-way, drain and cut in half.

Wrap bacon around scallop and put on skewer.

Place scallops in broiler or on a grill and baste with marinade while turning scallops. Cook until scallops are tender.

CRABMEAT MORNAY

1 Stick Butter
½ C Onions, chopped
¼ C Parsley, chopped
2 T Flour
1 Pt. Cream
½ lb. Swiss Cheese, grated
¼ C Sherry
1 lb. White Crabmeat
  Salt and Pepper, to Taste

Saute onions and parsley in butter.

Add flour, cream and cheese and cook until cheese has melted.

Add sherry, crabmeat and salt and pepper and simmer.

Pour ingredients in pastry shells or over toast and serve.

Serves six.

CURRIED CRABMEAT SALAD

2 lbs. Fresh or Canned Crabmeat
5 Celery Stalks, diced
2 C Mayonnaise
1 t Horseradish
2 Cans Mandarin Oranges, drained
1-2 T Curry Powder
  Salt and Pepper, to taste
1 Can Walnuts or Pecans, chopped
  Asparagus, Artichoke Hearts or Hard Boiled Eggs

Combine crabmeat, celery, mayonnaise, horseradish, oranges, curry powder, salt, pepper and walnuts.

Serve with asparagus, artichoke hearts or hard boiled eggs.

Serves eight.

EASY CRAB IMPERIAL

1 Green Pepper, finely diced
2 Pimentos, chopped
1 T English Mustard
1 T Salt
½ t White Pepper
2 Eggs
1 C Mayonnaise
3 lbs. Lump Crabmeat (backfin)
Dash of Paprika

Combine first seven ingredients.

Add crabmeat, mixing well with your fingers to prevent breaking crab lumps.

Place on individual shells, topping lightly with mayonnaise and adding paprika.

Bake at 350° for 15 minutes or until mayonnaise browns.

May be served hot or cold.

Serves nine to twelve.

CRABMEAT AND ARTICHOKE CASSEROLE

1 Stick of Butter
3 T Flour
1 C Cream
2/3 C Parmesan Cheese
1/2 t Worcestershire Sauce
1 t Salt
1 t Pepper
1 t Dry Mustard
1 lb. Can Artichoke Hearts or 1 box Frozen Artichokes, defrosted
2 C Crabmeat

Melt butter in large skillet and add flour and cream slowly, stirring constantly to make a white sauce.

Add half of the cheese and salt, pepper, Worcestershire Sauce, mustard and paprika.

Add artichoke and crabmeat and pour into a baking dish, sprinkling remainder of cheese on top.

Bake at 350° for 30 minutes.

Serves six.

SHRIMP SALAD

1 C Mayonnaise or Horseradish Dressing
½t Paprika
2 C Shrimp, chopped
2 Cantaloupes, hollowed out and shaped into balls
Whole Shrimp and Parsley, to garnish

Combine mayonnaise, paprika, shrimp and cantaloupe balls.

Garnish with whole shrimp and parsley.

Serves four.

GARLIC SHRIMP

¾ C Butter
¼ C Onions, finely chopped
3 T Garlic, finely chopped
2 lbs. Scampi or Large Shrimp, shelled and washed
1 t Salt
½ t Pepper
2 T Lemon Juice
¼ C Parsley

Saute shrimp in butter, onion and garlic for 5 to 8 minutes, turning shrimp once.

Transfer shrimp to hot platter or serving shells.

Add salt, pepper and lemon juice to butter in skillet.

Heat butter mixture, pour over shrimp and sprinkle with parsley.

Serves six.

SPICY SHRIMP AND EGGPLANT

1¼ lbs. Eggplant, cut into 1-inch cubes
1 C Seasoned Bread Crumbs
   Salt and Pepper, to taste
¾ C Olive Oil
3 C Canned Tomatoes, drained
1 C Onions, sliced (frozen may be used)
1 C Green Peppers, sliced (frozen may be used)
1½ lbs. Shrimp
1 T Parsley
1 T Garlic Powder
4 t Thyme
1 t Fines Herbes

Preheat oven to 375°.

Dredge eggplant in bread crumbs to which salt and pepper have been added.

Heat part of olive oil and saute eggplant until brown.

Add tomatoes and simmer for 10 minutes.

Add salt, pepper and seasonings.

In a separate skillet, saute shrimp in oil until pink.

Combine all ingredients in a baking dish, adding remainder of bread crumbs on top.

Bake for 10 minutes, then place under broiler for a few seconds.

Serves six.

EASY BOUILLABAISSE

¾package of frozen Green or Red Peppers (or 3 fresh ones, chopped)
½package of frozen Onions (or 2 chopped fresh ones)
1 T Garlic Powder
¼C Olive Oil
2 T Parsley
4 pounds of frozen Lobster Tails, Shrimps, Scallops, and Fish Fillets (or whatever fish you prefer)
Mussels or Clams in their shells (optional)
1 large can of Tomatoes
1½ C white wine
Salt and Lemon Pepper to taste
1 Bay Leaf
2½ C bottled clam juice
½t Thyme

In a large pot, saute onions, peppers, and garlic powder lightly.

Add the tomatoes, clam juice, wine, salt, pepper, parsley, thyme, and bay leaf. Simmer about fifteen minutes.

Add the seafood, cover, and simmer about 25 minutes longer.

Serves six.

SPICED PICKLED SHRIMP

2 lbs. Shrimp, cooked
  Bay Leaves (4 per layer)
1 C Onions, chopped
1 C Olive Oil
¼ C Tarragon Vinegar
2 t Salt
½ t Dry Mustard
1 t Sugar
1 t Worcestershire Sauce
1 t Cayenne Pepper
1 t Pickling Spice

In a large casserole, place layers of shrimp, bay leaves and onions.

Combine in a large bowl, oil, vinegar, salt, mustard, sugar, Worcestershire Sauce, pepper and pickling spice and pour over shrimp.

Cover and refrigerate for 2 hours, stirring occasionally.

May be served with cocktails, with a dip or with lettuce, as a salad.

SHRIMP CURRY

1 Stick of Butter
1 C Onions, chopped
3 Oranges, juice and some peelings (or one can of oranges)
3 Lemons, juice and some peelings
1 Can Pineapple Chunks
1 Can Shrimp Soup
2 Apples, peeled and chopped (dried are fine)
1 T Salt
½ T Cayenne
4 T Flour
4 T Curry Powder
1 t Paprika
2 lbs. Shrimp, cooked

Saute onions in butter and add fruit juices.

Combine remainder of ingredients, stirring until well blended and hot. Serves six.

STEAK SCHIFFER

2 Filet Mignon or Strip Steaks
  Salt and Pepper, to Taste
1 Jar Marinated Artichokes, drained
½lb. Fresh Mushrooms, washed or 2 Jars Marinated Mushrooms
1 Stick of Butter
  Fine Herbs, to Taste

Broil steaks on one side in an aluminum pan with salt and pepper.

Turn steak and place artichokes and mushrooms along side it, adding pats of butter.

Continue to broil until steak is done to your liking.

Serves two.

VEAL VERONIQUE

1 lb. Scalapinne of Veal, cut into ¼ inch thick slices
6 T Butter
7 T Olive Oil
  Salt and Freshly Ground Pepper, to taste
7 T Lemon Juice
2 C Mushrooms
2 C Seedless Grapes

Using butter, saute veal on one side.

Turn veal and add lemon juice, olive oil, grapes and mushrooms.

Add salt and pepper to taste.

The veal can be cooked half through and then reheated at the last minute.

Serves four.

EASY LONDON BROIL

1 Stick Butter
2 Medium-Sized Onions, sliced (or ½ C Frozen Onions)
1 Pkg. Lipton Onion Soup Mix
½ C Madeira
2 T Oil
1 t Lemon Juice
2 t Garlic Powder
1 t Pepper
2 lbs. Flank Steaks, Scored

Melt butter in skillet and saute onions.

Add onion soup mix and Madeira and keep warm.

In a bowl mix oil, lemon juice, garlic powder and pepper and brush on meat.

Broil for about 5 minutes or until it reaches preferred doneness. Turn meat and broil another 5 minutes or so.

Slice meat thinly and serve with onion sauce.

Serves six.

EASY POT ROAST

4 lbs. Pot Roast, boned and rolled
1 T Garlic Powder
1 T Salt
1 T Pepper
1 T Italian Herbs
1 T Parsley
½C Dry Vermouth or Red Wine
1 Can New Potatoes, sauteed
1 Can Carrots, sauteed
2 Cans White Onions, sauteed

Preheat oven to 350°. Place large sheet of heavy-duty foil in a shallow pan, placing roast on top and season with all herbs.

Place roast uncovered under the broiler and brown on both sides.

Remove from broiler, add wine or vermouth and close foil tightly. Cook at 350° for 1½ hours.

Open foil and add vegetables. Close foil and cook for 1 to 1½ hours.

Open foil, pouring off juice and reserving for gravy.

Serve meat and vegetables with juice or gravy.

Serves six.

CHILI MIO

2 T Bacon Dripping or Other Fat
1½ lbs. Lean Ground Beef
1 Large Onion, chopped
1 Clove Garlic, chopped
½ C Water
¾ C California Burgundy, Claret or other Red Dinner Wine
1 Beef Bouillon Cube
1 T Cumin Seed
1 T Chili Powder
2 t Oregano
   Salt, to Taste
2 (No. 303) Cans Red Kidney Beans

Using bacon drippings in a large skillet, saute beef, onion and garlic until meat is no longer red. Stir meat with fork to break meat into small pieces.

Add water, wine, bouillon cube and seasonings and bring to a boil.

Simmer, stirring often for about 40 minutes, until mixture is moist, but no longer juicy.

Add undrained kidney beans; cover and simmer for 5 minutes.

Serve in heated soup bowls or individual casseroles.

Ideal for Sunday night supper with green salad and hot cheese-topped French bread.

Serves five or six.

PEPPERED STEAK WITH MUSHROOMS ITALIAN STYLE

¼ C Oil
1½ lbs. Green Pepper, cut into 1½" squares
1 Large Garlic Clove, slivered
3 t Salt
1 t Pepper
1½ t Oregano
½ C Butter
½ lb. Fresh Mushrooms, sliced
1 lb. Beef Tenderloin, Rib Eye, Veal or Pork Tenderloin, cut
   into 2" cubes
¼ C Sherry or Sauterne Wine
¼ C Tomato Paste
2 Medium Firm Tomatoes, cut into large pieces

In oil, saute green pepper and several slivers of garlic for 5 minutes, turning often.

Season with 1 t salt, ¼ t pepper and ½ t oregano; cover and steam for 5 minutes, turning several times. (Peppers should be crisply tender and still green.) Set aside.

In ¼ C butter, saute mushrooms and several slivers of garlic and cook for 3 minutes, turning often. Season with ½ t salt, ¼ t pepper and ½ t oregano. Pour mushrooms into peppers.

In ¼ C butter saute several slivers of garlic for 1 minute and add meat and cook for 2 minutes over moderately high heat on both sides until brown.

Season with 1¼ t salt, ½ t oregano, ¼ t pepper, sherry or sauterne and tomato paste. Cover and steam for 5 minutes, turning several times. Add tomatoes.

When ready to serve, cook vegetables only until heated through — do not overcook.

To serve, mound hot vegetables on platter, and arrange meat over vegetables, pouring sauce on top. Or meat may be combined with vegetables and mounded on platter.

MEAT BALLS IN BURGUNDY SAUCE

1 lb. Lean Ground Beef
1 lb. Lean Ground Pork
2 C Stale Bread, crumbled
2 Eggs, slightly beaten
1 Small Onion, minced
1 Garlic Clove, minced
2 t Salt
½ t Pepper
½ t Allspice
¼ C Milk
¼ C Drippings
1½ T Flour
½ C Water
1 C Burgundy
1 Beef Bouillon Cube

Mix meats and combine with bread, eggs, onions, garlic, seasonings and milk.

Make meat balls about 1" in diameter; then brown on all sides in drippings; remove from pan.

Blend in flour, water, burgundy and bouillon and cook, stirring constantly until thick and smooth.

Return meat balls to pan; cover and simmer for 30 minutes.

Serve with hot noodles.

Serves eight to ten.

BARBECUED RIBS

3 -4 lbs. Ribs
2 T Lemon Juice
1 Large onion, sliced
1 C Catsup
2 T Worcestershire sauce
1 t Chili powder
1 t Salt
2 dashes tabasco sauce
1 T sugar
½C Open Pit Barbeque sauce (Hickory Smoke flavor)

Cut ribs in serving pieces and brown in a skillet or dutch oven. Add 1 cup water to keep the ribs from burning and cook for 30 minutes, stirring occasionally over medium heat.

Combine all remaining ingredients and pour over ribs. Cook for another 15 minutes.

Transfer ribs to a shallow baking pan and broil for about 15 minutes, turning once.

BEEF STROGANOFF
(Shrimp or Chicken can be substituted)

2 lbs. Beef Filet, cut into ½" slices (boneless round or chuck can be used)
1 Stick of Butter
1 C Onions, sliced (frozen is fine)
1 T Garlic Powder
1 C Mushroom Soup
1 lb. Fresh Mushrooms or 2 jars
1 T Catsup or Tomato Sauce
1 t Salt
½ t Pepper
1 C Beef Boullion (if using chicken or shrimp use chicken bouillon)
½ C Red Wine (if using chicken or shrimp use white wine)
1 t Dried Dill
1 T Fines Herbes
1½ C Sour Cream
1 T Worchestershire Sauce

Melt 1 T butter in heavy skillet and saute beef lightly; remove from skillet.

Melt remainder of butter and saute onions, garlic and mushrooms (about 5 minutes); remove from skillet.

Add to skillet the soup, catsup, salt, pepper, boullion, dill, herbes, wine, worshestershire sauce and sour cream; stirring until smooth.

Add beef, onions and mushrooms and simmer until sauce thickens.

Serves six.

MAUDIE SCOTT'S STEAK

1½-2" Thick Boneless Sirloin (London Broil)
 1 t Garlic Salt
 1 t Lemon Pepper
 1 Bottle Chili Sauce
   Dash of Worchestershire Sauce

Line a shallow pan with foil and place meat on top.

Sprinkle meat with garlic salt, lemon pepper and add ½ bottle chili sauce.

Place meat under broiler, leaving door slightly ajar, and broil for 10 minutes.

Remove meat and turn, adding seasonings again and using remainder of chili sauce.

Sprinkle on a little Worchestershire sauce (too much would burn chili sauce).

If you like rare meat, check it after it has been in for 15 minutes all together.

Slice meat very thin and spoon on the "chili" gravy.

VEAL SCALLOPINI WITH MARSALA

½lb. Scallopini of Veal, sliced ¼ inch thick
    Flour for Dredging
    Salt and Pepper, to Taste
2 T Butter
2 T Olive Oil
¼ C Marsala Wine

Cut veal into 3 inch square cubes and place between sheets of wax paper and pound to flatten.

Blend flour with salt and pepper and coat veal lightly with flour.

Heat butter and olive oil in large skillet, adding veal and browning on all sides at a high heat for 4 to 6 minutes.

Transfer veal to two warm plates.

Add wine to the skillet and stir to dissolve particles in the pan.

Reduce heat slightly and pour equal amounts over each serving of veal.

Serves two.

AVOCADO VEAL

1 lb. Scallopini of Veal, cut into ¼ inch slices
4 T Butter
2 T Olive Oil
2 Avocadoes, cut into bite-size pieces
2 Tomatoes, cut into bite-size pieces
2 C Stroganoff Sauce
½C Gruyere Cheese, grated
  Salt and Pepper, to Taste

Using butter and oil, saute veal on both sides in a large skillet.

Place avocadoes and tomatoes on top.

Add stroganoff sauce and cheese and place under broiler for 5 minutes or until browned.

Serves four to six.

LORNA'S CASSEROLE

2 lb. Ground Beef
1 t Salt
1 Can Tomato Paste
1 Can Tomato Sauce
1 lb. Fresh mushrooms, sliced
4-5 C Egg Noodles, Fine
1-8oz. Cottage Cheese
1-8oz. Cream Cheese
½C Green Onions, chopped
½Green Pepper, chopped
¾C Red Wine

Cook first 5 ingredients. Cook noodles. Mix all cheeses, then add onions and peppers.

Place a layer of noodles in a greased casserole. Add a layer of cheese mixture, then a layer of meat sauce. Repeat process, ending with meat sauce. Pour red wine over all. Bake at 350 degrees for 20 minutes, covered then 35 minutes, uncovered.

VEAL PICCATA WITH LEMON

½lb. Scallopini of Veal, sliced ¼ inch thick
  Flour for Dredging
  Salt and Pepper, to Taste
2 T Butter
2 T Olive Oil
2 T Dry White Wine
2 T Lemon Juice
2 Slices of Lemon, thinly sliced
2 t Parsley, finely chopped

Cut veal into 3 inch square cubes and place between sheets of wax paper and pound to flatten.

Blend flour with salt and pepper and coat veal lightly with flour.

Heat butter and olive oil in large skillet, adding veal and browning on all sides. The cooking time should be from 4 to 6 minutes at high heat.

Pour off fat from skillet and return to heat, adding the wine.

Cook briefly until wine starts to evaporate and add lemon juice and parsley.

Place veal on a platter and serve with lemon slices.

Serves four.

VEAL FORESTIER

1½ lb. Thin Veal Cutlets
½ C Flour
¼ C Butter
½ lb. Mushrooms, washed and thinly sliced
½ t Salt
   Dash of Pepper
1/3C Dry Vermouth
1 t Lemon Juice
1 T Parsley Flakes

Sprinkle veal with flour and saute in hot butter until browned on both sides.

Place mushrooms on top of veal in skillet.

Sprinkle with salt, pepper and vermouth.

Cover and cook over low heat for 20 minutes or until veal is tender.

Add 1 T water, if mixture gets too dry.

Place on platter, sprinkle with lemon juice and parsley and serve.

Serves six.

WINE BRAISED PORK CHOPS

8 Thick Pork Chops, loin or shoulder
2 t Prepared Mustard
  Salt and Pepper, to taste
  Dried Dill or Sage, to taste
  Brown Sugar, to taste
6 Thin Lemon Slices
1 C Sauterne, Chablis or other White Dinner Wine
  Cornstarch

Trim fat from chops, using fat to grease skillet.

Brown chops slowly on both sides, draining off excess fat.

Spread mustard on chops and sprinkling on top seasonings and brown sugar.

Place lemon slices on top of chops, and pour in wine. Cover and cook very slowly until tender, 50 to 60 minutes.

Remove chops to hot plate. Skim off fat from drippings and add cornstarch and water to thicken.

Spoon sauce over meat. Good with cranberry sauce.

Serves six.

RACK OF LAMB

  Rack of Lamb
1 Garlic Clove or ½ Onion
2 T Olive Oil
1 T Lemon Juice
½ C Dry White Wine or Very Dry Sherry

Rub lamb with garlic or onion.

Bake in hot oven at 350°, allowing 30 minutes to the pound and baste occasionally with drippings and added olive oil, lemon juice and wine or sherry.

ORANGE BAKED HAM SLICE

1 Center Cut Ham Slice, 1 to 1½" thick
1 T Instant Minced Onion or ¼ C finely chopped raw onion
2 Medium-Sized Oranges
¼ C Brown Sugar (packed)
1 Medium-Sized Lemon, sliced
½ C Sauterne, Chablis or other White Dinner Wine

Score ham fat on edges to prevent curling, and place in baking dish.

Sprinkle onion over ham.

Peel and cut oranges into medium-thick slices and arrange on ham.

Sprinkle brown sugar on top.

Place lemon slices on top and pour wine over all.

Bake at 375º for ¾ to 1 hour or until ham is tender.

Serves four to six.

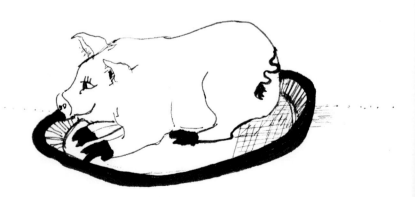

SCOTCH OR BOURBON GLAZED HAM STEAK

1 1-inch thick Ham Steak, Fully Cooked
2 T Brown Sugar
2 t Dijon Mustard
1/8 t Ginger Powder
5 T Scotch or Bourbon
1 Orange, Sliced or Mandarin Oranges

Make a few cuts around steak to prevent curling.

Combine sugar, mustard, ginger and liquor to make a paste.

Warm the remaining liquor.

Broil ham steak for 5 minutes until browned. Turn and broil other side for 4 minutes.

Spread ham with paste and broil for one or two minutes until glazed. Add oranges.

Ignite liquor and pour flaming over the ham. Once the flames go out, slice and serve with the sauce and oranges.

Serves Two or Three.

STUFFED PORK CHOPS

4 T Butter
Apricot Stuffing (see recipe or any of the stuffing recipes will do)
4 1" thick, Pork Chops, sliced with a pocket on the side of each
Salt, Pepper and Garlic Salt, to Taste

Stuff each pork chop with stuffing mixture and season with herbs.

Saute pork shops in butter and cook in a covered skillet for 1 hour over a low heat or until tender.

Garnish with spiced crabapples and parsley.

IN-A-HURRY LAMB CHOPS

Thick Lamb Chops
Whole Tomatoes, fresh or canned
1 C Dry Dinner Wine, Red or White
Salt and Pepper, to taste
Butter

Brown lamb chops in butter in a skillet.

Add tomatoes, and cook covered for 10 minutes.

Before serving, add wine, salt, pepper and heat.

Top each chop and tomato with butter.

RED WINE CURRY

1 Stick of butter or margarine
2 lbs. of boneless Lamb Cubes
1 package of frozen Chopped Onions
1 package of dried Apples
1 package of dried Apricots
1 t Garlic Powder
2 T Flour
2 T Hot Curry Powder
1½ t Ground Ginger
1 t Salt (seasoned is best)
1 C Beef Boullon
1 C Red Wine
1 t Lemon Juice
1 t Lemon Pepper

Melt butter and brown lamb cubes. Add onions, apples, apricots and garlic to meat. Sprinkle with flour, curry powder and all other ingredients. Simmer for two hours and taste to correct seasonings if you desire.

Serve with rice or barley with curry condiments.

Serves 4 - 6.

PARSLEYED RACK OF LAMB

½ to 2 lbs. Rack of Lamb or Leg of Lamb
  Jane's Krazy Salt and Pepper, to Taste
½ t Garlic Powder
1 Stick Butter, Melted
1 C Bread Crumbs
¼ C Fresh Parsley, Chopped
¼ t Thyme
¼ t Rosemary

Season lamb with salt, pepper and garlic powder.

Roast in oven at 325⁰ for ½ hour (Check roasting chart for the amount of time required according to weight and how well done you like your lamb.)

Combine butter, bread crumbs, parsley, thyme and Rosemary to make the paste.

About 30 minutes before done, remove lamb from oven and press the paste firmly onto the top surface of the lamb.

Return lamb to oven and bake 30 minutes longer or until coating turns golden brown.

Serve lamb with sprigs of parsley.

BURGUNDY LAMB WITH CRANBERRY-ORANGE SAUCE

    2 lbs. Lean Lamb, cut into 1" cubes
1/3 C Flour
    1 Stick Butter
    1 C Onion, chopped
    1 T Garlic Powder
    1 t Salt
    1 t Pepper
    1 (6 oz.) Can Tomato Paste
2½ C Burgundy Wine
1/2 t Ginger
1/2 t Oregano
    1 C Orange-Cranberry Sauce
    4 C Cooked Rice

Dip lamb in flour and saute in butter in a large covered pot.

Add onion, garlic, salt, pepper, tomato paste and burgundy. Cover and cook at medium heat for 45 minutes.

Add ginger, oregano and cranberry sauce, cooking another 45 minutes or until meat is tender.

Serve over hot cooked rice.

Serves six.

POULTRY

STS

SURPRISE CHICKEN

8 Chicken Breasts, deboned
2 Sticks Butter
1 to 2 t Garlic Powder
1 t Paprika
1-½ Pkgs. Lipton's Onion Soup Mix
1 to 2 Jiggers of Brandy

Remove the skin from chicken breasts and place in a casserole which has a lid.

Melt the butter, garlic, paprika and onion soup mix in a sauce pan, and pour mixture over the chicken, making sure that all pieces are covered.

Bake covered at 325° for 1 hour. Then remove lid, pour in brandy and continue to cook another 20 minutes without a lid.

No one will be able to tell how you made this delicious and easy chicken dish.

Serves eight.

LEMON CHICKEN WITH MUSHROOMS

6 T Butter
6 Large Chicken Breasts
6 T Olive Oil
7 T Lemon Juice
1 t Garlic Powder
Salt and Pepper, to Taste
2 C Sliced Mushrooms
1/3 C Parsley

Using butter, oil and seasonings, saute chicken on one side.

Turn and saute chicken on other side adding parsley and mushrooms.

Serves Six.

ORANGE CHICKEN

 6 Chicken Breasts, deboned
 4 T Olive Oil
 1 Garlic Clove, sliced
 2 Medium Onions, sliced
 2 Bay Leaves
12 Black Peppercorns
 2 C White Wine
 ½ C Cointreau
 1 Lemon, sliced
 2 Oranges, sliced
   Salt, to taste

Saute chicken in olive oil.

Add all other ingredients and simmer until done.

Serves six.

CHICKEN AMBASSADOR

6 to 8 Lg. Chicken Breasts
1 T Salt
1 t Poultry Seasoning
 Dash of Paprika
½C Melted Butter
1 Can Beef Consomme
½C Sherry
½lb. Fresh Mushrooms, washed and sliced
2.(10 oz.) Cans Artichoke Hearts

Season chicken with salt, seasoning and paprika and place in a roasting pan, skin side up.

Combine butter and consomme and baste chicken.

Bake at 325° for 1 hour, basting every 20 minutes.

Saute mushrooms in butter.

Remove chicken to heated plates and combine drippings in pan with mushrooms and artichoke hearts. Heat sauce and pour over chicken.

Serves six.

BERNAISE CHICKEN

4 Chicken Breasts, cut into bite-size chunks
1 Stick of Butter
2 oz. Dried Shallots or Chives
2 oz. Parsley
   Krazy Jane Salt and Pepper, to taste
¼ t Garlic Powder
¼ t Mustard Powder
   Few dashes of Lemon Juice
8 oz. Fresh Cream
3 oz. Bernaise Sauce
1 Pkg. Cooked Rice (wild or seasoned is best)

Melt butter in a large skillet until slightly brown.

Add shallots and parsley and saute.

Add salt, pepper, garlic and mustard and stir.

Add chicken and cook until tender, but not brown.

Add lemon juice, cream and Bernaise sauce and stir over a low flame for 2 to 3 minutes; making sure it does not curdle.

Serve with rice.

(The chicken can be cooked before the guests arrive and kept warm. Then just add the Bernaise sauce, cream and lemon juice at the last minute.)

Serves four.

SWISS CHICKEN

4 Large Chicken Breasts, Boned
4 Large Slices Swiss Cheese
4 Slices Ham or Canadian Bacon
  Bread Crumbs, Olive Oil, Salt and Pepper, to Taste

Slice side of chicken breasts lengthwise.

Place 1 slice each of cheese and ham in each chicken breast.

Dip chicken in olive oil (in flat pan) and then in bread crumbs (in flat pan).

Place chicken in flat pan, breast-side up.

Cook for 1 hour at 400°.   Serves four.

TONY'S CHICKEN CHUTNEY

  4 lbs. Cooked White Chicken or Turkey, diced into chunks
1½ C Mayonnaise
  1 C Raisins
  1 C Salted Peanuts
  1 C Mango Chutney
  1 C Coconut
    Salt and Pepper, to taste
  2 C Bananas, sliced lengthwise
    Salad Greens
    Avocados, sliced and dipped in lemon or lime juice

Mix all the ingredients, except for the last three which are for decoration.

Place salad greens on a large platter and mound mixture in the center.

Decorate with slices of avocados and bananas.

Serves ten to twelve.

CHICKEN FLORENTINE

3 Pkgs. Frozen Spinach
3 Sticks Butter
   Salt, Pepper and Nutmeg, to Taste
2½ C Heavy Cream
2 T Olive Oil
6 Chicken Breasts, skinned and boned
1 C Gruyere Cheese mixed with Parmesan Cheese (both freshly grated) or use 1 pkg. Cheese Fondue Mix

Cook spinach according to directions and add 1 stick of butter and salt and pepper, to taste. Add ½ C cream.

Simmer mixture, stirring until cream is almost absorbed.

Add 1 C more of cream, stirring slowly as before.

Season with salt, pepper and nutmeg, to taste.

Saute chicken in 2 sticks of butter and olive oil for 10 minutes.

Place spinach in a buttered casserole dish, putting chicken on top. Add the remainder of the cream and sprinkle cheese on top.

Place dish under broiler for 3 to 5 minutes or until the cheese is melted and the sauce is lightly browned.

Serves six.

SAUCY CHICKEN

3 to 4 lbs. Chicken, cut up
1 Bottle Catalina Salad Dressing
1 (8 oz.) Jar Apricot Jam
1 Envelope Lipton Onion Soup Mix
1 C White or Rose Wine

Combine in a bowl the salad dressing, wine, jam and onion soup mix, stir well.

Place chicken in a baking pan and pour sauce on top.

Bake at 350° for 1¼ hour. (No need to turn.)

Serves four.

PARMESAN CHICKEN

1 C Butter, melted
¼ C Parmesan Cheese, grated
1 C Progresso Italian Bread Crumbs
2 t Parsley
1 t Salt
1 t Garlic Powder
1 t Pepper
½ t Thyme
½ t Oregano
4 Chicken Breasts

Preheat oven to 375°.

Combine first nine ingredients in a saucepan and pour over chicken which has been placed in a flat pan.

Bake for 1 hour or until chicken is golden brown.
Serves four.

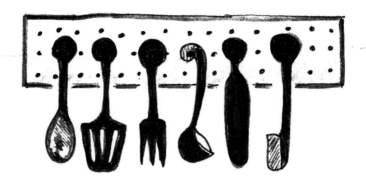

BOURBON OR SCOTCH CHICKEN

1 Stick Butter
2 T Oil
4 Chicken Breasts, Skinned and Boned
1 Medium-Sized Onion, finely chopped
¼ lb. Mushrooms, sliced
½ C Bourbon or Scotch
½ C Chicken Broth
1 C Sour Cream
2 T Fines Herbs
   Salt and Pepper, to Taste

Heat butter and oil in large skillet. Saute chicken over medium heat, turning often until it is golden brown on both sides.

Add onion and mushrooms. Cook until softened.

Pour the liquor into the pan and ignite.

When flames go out, add broth, cover skillet and reduce heat.

Simmer about 25 minutes or until chicken is tender. Remove chicken and keep warm.

Reduce heat to very low and stir in sour cream. Thoroughly heat and add fines herbs, salt and pepper to taste.

Pour over chicken.

Serves four.

CHICKEN IN HERBED SOUR CREAM

8 Small Chicken Breasts, skinned and boned
  Salt and Pepper, to Taste
1 t Garlic
1 t Thyme
1 t Parsley
1 Bay Leaf
1 Stick Butter
1 C Dry White Wine
5 Egg Yolks
1 C Sour Cream
  Juice of half of Lemon

Season chicken with first five ingredients.

Saute chicken lightly in ½ stick of butter (do not brown).

Add wine and simmer until chicken is tender.

Remove chicken to a warm platter.

Beat together the egg yolks and sour cream, adding the mixture to the skillet and cooking slowly until it thickens. (Do not let boil.)

Stir in lemon and remaining butter, adding more salt and pepper, to taste.

Return chicken to skillet and heat. Sprinkle paprika on top and serve.

Serves eight.

LEMON CHICKEN I

2 Chickens, cut into pieces
1 C Olive Oil
½C Lemon Juice (3 lemons)
2 T Oregano
3 Garlic Cloves, minced
  Salt and Pepper, to Taste

Place chicken in a baking dish.

Combine in a bowl and mix well the olive oil, lemon juice, oregano, garlic, salt and pepper. Pour over chicken and marinate for 2 hours.

Preheat oven to 350°. Place chicken skin side down in marinade and bake for 30 to 40 minutes until chicken is done.

Remove chicken and place under broiler until skin is crisp and brown.

Chicken can be kept in a 200° oven for 1 hour before serving. Pour pan juices over chicken before serving.

(You can also grill the chicken over a charcoal fire by placing the marinated chicken in heavy foil that has been perforated every inch or so. Baste chicken occasionally.)

LEMON CHICKEN II

  Juice of 2 Lemons
1 T Garlic Powder
4 T Soy Sauce
4 T Honey
4 Chicken Breasts, skinned, deboned and split

Combine first four ingredients, mixing well.

Place chicken in marinade for 1 hour.

Broil chicken for 15 minutes.

ROSEMARY'S 10-MINUTE CHICKEN

4 Lg. Chicken Breasts
2 Sticks Butter or Margarine
1 Box of Fresh Mushrooms, washed or 2 cans
1 t Tarragon
1 t Fines Herbes
   Salt and Pepper, to taste

Slice chicken lengthwise and spread with butter.

Sprinkle salt, pepper and herbs over chicken and broil in butterfly fashion for 4 minutes on each side, making sure that both sides are buttered and seasoned.

Before the final 2 minutes of broiling, place mushrooms and seasoned butter drippings inside the cavity and continue broiling for 2 or 3 more minutes.

Serves four.

MUSTARD CHICKEN I

   Chicken Breasts, boned and flattened (use 1 breast per person)
   Dijon Mustard, to Taste
   Bread Crumbs, Plain
   Parmesan Cheese Mix
6 T Butter

Spread Dijon Mustard on chicken breasts.

Combine bread crumbs and Parmesan Cheese Mix and bread chicken breasts.

Saute chicken in butter until done; 5 to 10 minutes at most.

MUSTARD CHICKEN II
(Veal can also be used)

2 Chickens (2½ to 3 lbs Broilers, Quartered)
7 T Butter
7 C Dry White Wine
½t Dried Tarragon
  Pinch of Thyme
1 Small Bay Leaf
1 t Salt
1 t Pepper
7 Egg Yolks
6 T Sour Cream
6 T Dijon Mustard
  Pinch Cayenne Pepper

Melt butter in skillet. Add chicken and cook until browned well on both sides.

Add wine, tarragon, thyme, bay leaf, salt and pepper.

Bring to boil, then cover and simmer 45 minutes until chicken is tender.

Remove chicken to heated serving dish to keep warm.

Discard bay leaf.

Blend sauce with egg yolks.

Add sour cream, mustard and pepper.

Heat, stirring briskly and constantly. Do not allow to boil.

Pour over chicken.

Serves eight.

CHUTNEY CHICKEN

6 Chicken Breasts
3 T Butter
½C Currant Jelly
½C Chutney
2 T Dry Sherry
1 t Salt
1 (6 oz.) Pkg. Seasoned Long-Grain & Wild Rice
½t Curry Powder

In large skillet, saute chicken in butter on both sides, adding salt.

Cover and cook over low heat for 30 minutes and drain off fat.

In a small bowl, combine jelly, chutney and sherry and pour over chicken.

Cover and simmer 10 to 15 minutes until tender, basting occasionally.

If thicker sauce is desired, simmer uncovered for a few minutes.

Prepare rice according to directions and stir in curry powder.

Serve rice with chutney chicken.

Serves six.

VIRGINIA KNAUER'S CHICKEN ZETA

1 Jar Russian Dressing
1 Pkg. Lipton's Onion Soup Mix
1 7-8 oz. Jar Apricot Jam
½C Red Wine
½C Slivered Almonds (optional)
½C Raisins
    Chicken Pieces (approximately 3 lbs. of breasts and legs)
    Salt, to taste

Wash chicken pieces and drain. Place chicken in Dutch Oven and add salt.

Combine the first six ingredients in a saucepan and heat at low flame until mixture is combined well.

Pour half of the "Zeta" mixture over chicken, reserving the rest to be served in a sauce boat.

Bake chicken at 350° for 1 to 1½ hours.

Lift chicken from broth and arrange on platter with parsley. Pour hot broth over chicken.

Serve with herb rice.

Serves four to six.

CHICKEN TETRAZZINI

6 Chicken Breasts (or 2 lbs. of canned chicken)
¼ lb. Wide Egg Noodles
½ lb. Fresh Mushrooms
¼ lb. Parmesan Cheese
1 stick of Butter or Margarine

SAUCE

¼ C Butter
1/3 C Flour
2 C Milk
1 C Chicken Stock
2 T Sauterne wine
½ t Salt

If using fresh chicken, saute in 4 T of butter and then cut into slivers. Otherwise, just open the cans.

Boil noodles in unsalted water for 10 minutes, then rinse with cold water and add 1 t salt and 2 T melted butter and 2 T Parmesan Cheese. Set aside.

Saute mushrooms in 2 T butter, ½ t salt and pepper. Cook cream sauce.

In buttered casserole, place alternate layers of noodle, mushroom, chicken slices, sauce and cheese. There should be about 4 layers in all, ending with cheese. Bake for 30 minutes at 350 degrees.

Serves 6.

RICE WITH CHICKEN
(ARROZ CON POLLO)

1 disjointed Fryer (approx. 3 lbs.)
½ C Olive or Salad Oil
1 Medium Onion, chopped (frozen is fine)
1¼ t Salt
1/8t Pepper
½ t Garlic Powder
1 Bay Leaf
3 C Canned Tomatoes
1 C Raw Rice
¾ t Salt
6 Pimiento Stuffed Olives
1 Green Pepper (frozen is fine)

Cook chicken gently in hot oil until lightly browned, turning pieces occasionally. Add onion and cook until transparent. Add salt, pepper, garlic, bay leaf and tomatoes which have been heated to boiling.

Wash rice in sieve, drain and add to above mixture. Sprinkle ¾ t salt over surface, cover and cook over low heat for 30 to 40 minutes. Stir rice once after 15 or 20 minutes. Rice should be fluffy and tender and liquid absorbed. Remove garlic and bay leaf and turn onto warm platter or bowl.

Garnish with slices of olives and green pepper rings.

Serves 5 or 6.

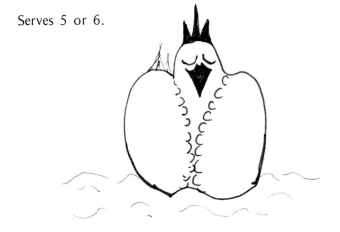

CHICKEN WITH PORT

1 stick Butter or Margarine
6 Chicken Breasts
¼ C Brandy
1 C Port
1 C Water
1 C Whipping Cream
4 large Carrots
10 fresh Mushrooms or 1 can mushrooms
½ t Tarragon
    Salt and Pepper, to Taste

Saute the chicken breasts in butter until golden brown. Flambe the chicken with the brandy.

Add salt, pepper and tarragon. Add carrots and mushrooms. Add port and water. Simmer for 45 minutes.

Add cream and simmer for 10 minutes, do not boil. Serve with noodles or a rice pilaf.

Serves six.

CONGO CURRY CHICKEN

6 Chicken Breasts
2 sticks of Butter or Margarine
1 T Curry Powder (or more if you like hot curry)
4 T Chunky Peanut Butter
1 can of Curry Soup
   Salt and Pepper to Taste
1 t Ginger (optional)
1 large can of Pineapple Chunks (optional)

Saute the chicken in the butter until it is browned, on all sides, about fifteen minutes.

Add all other ingredients and simmer for about fourty minutes. Serve with chutney and some other curry condiments. (eg. coconut, sliced bananas, peanuts, sliced eggs, and raisins). Serves six.

CHICKEN COOKED IN BEER

6 Chicken Breasts
1 T Garlic Powder
½package of frozen Onions or 2 large Onions, chopped
2 sticks of Butter or Margarine
¼ C Seasoned Bread Crumbs
2 C Beer
1 C Heavy Cream
   Salt and Pepper, to Taste

Roll the chicken in the bread crumbs. Saute it with the onions and garlic for about fifteen minutes or until it is brown on all sides.

Place the chicken in a casserole, season to taste, and pour 1 cup of beer over it. Bake for about half an hour at 350° or until cooked, occasionally basting with the rest of the beer.

When the chicken is done, add the cream and stir until it is warm. Serves six.

EMILY RICE'S DUCK A L'ORANGE

2 Oranges, grate rind and strain juice or use frozen orange juice
1 Duck, quartered
1 Lemon, strain juice
2 T Sugar
2 T Brandy
  Cornstarch
  Water

Place quartered duck skin-side up on a baking rack. Prick entire skin with a needle to allow fat to escape.

Bake duck at 350° for about one hour, basting with orange sauce. Serves four.

ORANGE SAUCE

In a saucepan add orange juice, orange rind, lemon juice, sugar and brandy, and bring to a boil.

Add just enough cornstarch and water to slightly thicken.

CHICKEN A' L'ORANGE

1 Stick Butter
1 t Salt
1 t Pepper
1 t Paprika
2 T Orange Rind, slivered
2 Cans Mandarin Oranges
2 T Flour
1 T Brown Sugar
½t Ginger
1 t Fines Herbs
1 Chicken, cut up

Add herbs to butter and saute chicken.

Add Mandarin oranges and its juice.

Add remaining ingredients.

Cover and simmer over low heat for 45 minutes or until chicken is tender.   Serves four.

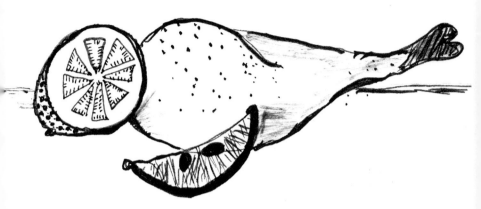

EASY TURKEY CURRY

1 Canned Turkey Breast, cooked
4 T Butter
2 Medium Onions, sliced (frozen is fine)
2 Medium Apples, sliced (dried is fine)
4 T Raisins
2 T Curry Powder
2 T Flour
4 T Major Grey's Chutney
2 C Chicken Boullion
1 t Lemon Juice
2 t Sugar
1 C Pineapple Juice or Pineapple Chunks

Heat turkey and cut into cubes.

Saute onions and apples in butter.

Add raisins, curry powder, flour, chutney and sugar.

Add stock gradually, mixing well.

Add lemon juice and simmer ½ hour, adding pineapple juice or chunks.

GRAND MARNIER OR BRANDY DUCKLING

1 t Salt
1 t Pepper
1 t Parsley
1 Bay Leaf
¼ t Allspice
½ C each of Brandy and Claret or (use 1 C Grand Marnier)
1 4 to 5 lb. Duck, quartered
6 Strips of Bacon
1 T Garlic Powder
2 C Mushrooms, washed and sliced

Combine first six ingredients and marinate duck at least five hours or overnight.

Place duck in covered roasting pan, placing the bacon on top.

Pour marinade over duck and bacon, adding the garlic powder.

Simmer for 1½ to 2 hours or until duck is tender.

Add mushrooms and cook for 5 minutes or until mushrooms are fully heated.

(Two cans of drained Mandarin oranges may be added for zest.)

Serves four.

VEGETABLES

MUSHROOM-SPINACH SOUFFLE

3 Boxes Stouffers Spinach Souffle
(Other is OK, but Stouffers is best)
1 lb. Fresh Mushrooms, Washed and Sliced
½ Stick of Butter
Salt, Pepper and Italian Herbs, to Taste

Cook spinach souffle according to directions.

Meanwhile, in a large skillet saute mushrooms in butter for 2 or 3 minutes. Add salt, pepper and Italian Herbs.

When ready to serve spinach souffle, pour it into the skillet used to cook mushrooms, and mix and serve.

Serves six generously.

CAULIFLOWER AND BROCCOLI AU-GRATIN

1   Pkg. Stouffers Broccoli Au Gratin
1   Pkg. Stouffers Cauliflower Au Gratin

Prepare both vegetables according to directions.

After cooking, combine vegetables and serve.

SEASONED ARTICHOKE HEARTS

1 can of Artichoke Hearts in brine, drained
1 C of seasoned Italian Bread Crumbs (or ½ C normal bread
    crumbs, ½ C parmesan cheese, and 1 T Italian Herbs)
1 Egg, lightly beaten
1 stick of Butter or Margarine

Dip the artichokes in the egg and then the bread crumb mixture. Saute them in butter for about five minutes and then serve.

Serves four.

ARTICHOKES AND PEAS

2 Jars Marinated Artichokes, Drained or 1 Can Artichoke Hearts
1 Stick Butter
2 T Olive Oil
1/3 C Bacon Bits
1/2 Small Onion, Minced
1/4 C Parsley
1/2 t Garlic Powder
1/2 t Dried Basil
   Salt and Pepper, to Taste
1/3 C Chicken Bouillon
2 Pkgs. Frozen Peas, Thawed

Heat half the butter and all the oil in a heavy casserole or pan.

Add the herbs, bacon and onion. Saute for several minutes.

Add artichokes and bouillon.

Lower heat and simmer for about 10 minutes, covered.

Add the peas and rest of the butter (add more bouillon, if needed).

Cover and simmer for 5 to 10 minutes longer or until both vegetables are tender.

Serves Six.

EASY BROILED TOMATOES

1 Tomato
1 Slice Red or White Onion
1 t Dijon Mustard
½t Sugar

Mix sugar and mustard.

Place on top of onion on top of sliced tomato.

Broil until tomato is soft and mixture is bubbling.

GRAND MARNIER CARROTS

3 Pkgs. Bird seye Brown Sugar-Glaze Carrots
½ Stick of Butter
3 T Fresh or Dried Mint
3½ T Grand Marnier

Cook carrots as directed, but add to the butter, Grand Marnier and mint.

Add pepper to taste.

Just before serving, a dash more of Grand Marnier may be added, if you like it.

Serves four to six.

MUSHROOM BROCCOLI

2 Pkgs. Frozen Broccoli
1 (10 oz.) Can Cream of Mushroom Soup
2 T Lemon Juice
Salt and Pepper, to Taste
2/3 C Cheddar Cheese, grated

Cook broccoli according to directions, drain and place in a shallow serving dish.

Combine soup, lemon juice and salt and pepper and pour over broccoli.

Sprinkle cheese on top and place under broiler for 10 minutes or until cheese bubbles.

Serves six.

HERBED GREEN BEANS

2 Pkgs. Frozen Green Beans
2 T White Wine Vinegar
1 t Dry Mustard
1 t Ground Cumin
1 t Salt
1 t Pepper
1 T Chopped Shallots
6 T Olive Oil
2 Cans Water Chestnuts (optional)

Cook beans according to directions and drain.

Combine all other ingredients and serve over beans which may be hot or cold.

Serves six.

BAKED CAULIFLOWER

1 Head of Cauliflower
1 Stick of Butter
2 T Flour
1 C Milk
1 t Salt
1 t Pepper
1 t Paprika
½ C Onions, chopped (frozen is fine)
½ C Seasoned Bread Crumbs

Add salt to boiling water and cook cauliflower for 20 minutes and drain and place in a baking dish.

Melt butter in a saucepan and saute onions.

Add flour, milk, salt, pepper, paprika, and bread crumbs, stirring until blended.

Pour sauce over cauliflower and bake at 375° for 20 minutes or until browned. Serves four.

MUSHROOMS IN SOUR CREAM

1 Stick of Butter
¼ C Onions, chopped
1 lb. Fresh Mushrooms, washed and dried
1 C Sour Cream
¼ C Sherry
1 t Salt
1 t Pepper
1 t Fines Herbs

Saute onions in butter.

Add mushrooms and cook at low heat for 5 minutes.

Ad remaining ingredients and simmer until heated.

Serves six.

FRENCH FRIED CAULIFLOWER OR BROCCOLI

1 Medium Head Cauliflower or Broccoli
2 Eggs, Beaten
¼ C Water
¼ t Fines Herbs
¼ t Jane's Krazy Salt
¼ t Pepper
½ C All Purpose Flour
1 C Bread Crumbs
  Oil for Frying

Wash vegetables and separate into serving pieces.

Cook in boiling, salted water until barely tender.

Drain and cool to room temperature.

To make batter, combine eggs, water and seasonings, and stir well.

Roll vegetable lightly in flour. Dip into batter and place on wire rack to drain. Roll in bread crumbs.

Deep fry in 360° oil for 1 minute or until golden brown.

Drain on absorbent paper and sprinkle lightly with salt.

Serve at once.

Serves four to six.

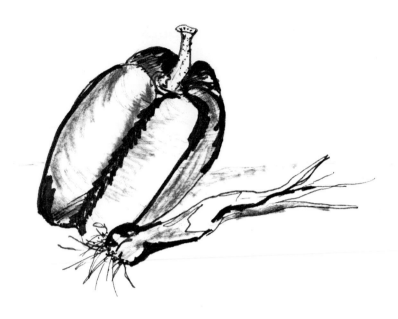

HERBED SQUASH

2 lbs. Summer Squash, sliced
2 C Water
2 Sticks Butter
1 t Crazy Jane Salt
1 t Pepper
1 T A-1 Sauce
3 T Chives
1 T Italian Herbs

Combine squash, water, 1 stick of butter, seasonings and A-1 Sauce in sauce pan and cover. Heat at low temperature for about 20 minutes.

Five minutes before completion of cooking, add chives and 1 stick of butter.

Serves seven.

BRUSSELS SPROUTS AND CHESTNUTS

2 (10 oz.) Pkgs. Frozen Brussels Sprouts
1 Stick Butter
1 T Parsley
½ t Thyme
   Salt and Pepper, to Taste
1 (5 oz.) Can Waterchestnuts

Cook brussels sprouts according to package instructions.

Add butter, seasonings and chestnuts and mix well.

Serves six.

SEASONED SQUASH

3 lbs. Squash
1 Stick Butter
1 C Sour Cream
1 C Onion, finely chopped
1 t Garlic Powder
   Crazy Jane Salt and Pepper, to Taste
1 T Fines Herbs
1 C Parmesan Cheese (optional)

Cut squash into bite-size pieces, removing seeds and other rot.

Place squash in a covered pan of boiling salted water (½ t salt and 1 C water) for 15 to 20 minutes or until tender.

Drain.

Heat oven to 400°.

Mash or blend squash and stir in remaining ingredients. Place mixture in an ungreased 1 quart casserole.

Bake uncovered for 20 to 30 minutes.

Serve with Parmesan Cheese, if desired.

Serves six.

ONION AND MUSHROOM CASSEROLE

1 Stick Butter
1 t Fresh Lemon Juice
1½ C Mushrooms, washed
1 C White Sauce (commercial ones are fine)
1 Can Whole Onions, drained
½ C Sharp Cheddar Cheese, grated
½ C Bread Crumbs, seasoned
1 t Jane's Krazy Salt
1 t Pepper
1 t Fines Herbs

Saute mushrooms in ½ stick of butter and lemon juice.

Add white sauce and pour into a 1½ quart casserole.

Add onions and combine.

Cover and bake at 375° for 15 minutes.

Remove cover and sprinkle over mixture the bread crumbs, cheese, salt, pepper and herbs. Slice the remaining butter and place around the top of mixture.

Bake at 350° uncovered for 20 minutes or until the bread crumbs are brown and the cheese is melted.

Serves six.

ZUCCHINI WITH PARMESAN CHEESE

½C Sliced Onion
2 T Butter
½C Water
1 T Italian Dressing Mix
1 lb. Zucchini, thinly sliced
1 T Grated Parmesan Cheese

Saute onion slices in butter until lightly browned.

Add water, salad dressing and zucchini.

Cover and simmer in pan until tender.

Sprinkle with cheese and serve.

Serves five to eight.

CAULIFLOWER AND PEAS

½t Cumin
1 t Pepper
1 t Garlic Salt
¼t Coriander
1 t Tumeric
1 Stick Butter
1 Medium-Sized Onion, chopped
1 Bay Leaf
1 Lg. Head Cauliflower, Washed
1 Pkg. Frozen Peas
½C Water

Boil water, adding ½ stick of butter and all herbs.

Break cauliflower into florets and add to boiling water. Steam 15 to 20 minutes.

Cook peas as directed on package.

Add peas to cauliflower and mix with rest of butter.

Serves eight.

STRING BEANS OR PEAS

Jazz up frozen String Beans or Peas with either Toasted Almonds, Crisp Bacon Bits, Chopped Chives, Chopped Garlic or Garlic Salt, Fresh Mint or Curry Powder and with either Butter or Sour Cream.

BAKED ACORN SQUASH WITH APPLES

4 Medium-Sized Acorn Squash
½C Water
1 Lg. Can Sliced Apples
½C Light Brown Sugar
  Dash of Salt
1 Stick Butter, melted
2 T Cinnamon Sugar
1 t Nutmeg
  Juice of 1 Lemon

Preheat oven to 350°. Wash squash, cut in half lengthwise and scoop out seeds and membranes.

Place squash in baking pan, cut side down, adding water. Cover with foil and bake for 45 minutes.

Increase oven to 425° and drain squash.

Mix apples with ¼ C sugar, turn squash, sprinkling each with dash of salt and fill the cavities with apples.

Add butter, sugar, cinnamon and nutmeg on top.

Bake about 12 minutes or until apples are glazed.

Serves 8.

MUSHROOMS PROVENCAL

1 lb. Mushrooms, stems removed
4 T Butter
  Salt and Pepper, to Taste
1 T Chopped Shallots
1 Clove Garlic, crushed or 1 t Garlic Powder
  Chopped Parsley
1 t Fine Herbs

Wash and dry mushrooms.

Saute mushrooms in butter and add salt and pepper.

Add shallots and garlic and saute another few minutes.

Sprinkle in herbs and serve.

Serves four.

TOMATOES AU GRATIN

6 Large Ripe Tomatoes
1 t Salt
2 T Olive Oil
¼ t Black Pepper
2 T Parsley
2 t Oregano
1 Clove Garlic, minced or 1 t powdered
½ C Grated Parmesan Cheese
6 T Bread Crumbs
6 T Butter

Cut tomatoes in half and hull and sprinkle with salt.

Combine remainder of ingredients and place on a well-oiled pan.

Bake at 350⁰ for 15 minutes and baste with melted butter.

BROCCOLI SUPREME

1 Pkg. Frozen Broccoli, Thawed
1 t Marjoram
½ Can of Cream of Mushroom Soup
½ C Sour Cream
  Herb Seasoned Bread Crumbs, to Taste

Place broccoli in small baking dish and sprinkle with marjoram.

Mix soup and sour cream and spread over broccoli.

Top with bread crumbs.

Bake at 375° for 40 minutes or until tender.

Add water chestnuts, if desired.

Serves four to six.

BROCCOLI AU-GRATIN WITH MUSHROOMS

3 Boxes Stouffers Broccoli Au-Gratin
1 lb. Fresh Mushrooms, Washed and Sliced
½ Stick of Butter
  Salt, Pepper and Italian Herbs, to Taste

Cook the broccoli au-gratin according to directions.

Meanwhile, in a large skillet saute mushrooms in butter for 2 or 3 minutes. Add salt, pepper and Italian Herbs.

When ready to serve broccoli, pour it into the skillet used to cook mushrooms, and mix and serve.

Serves six generously.

ZUCCHINI CHEESE CASSEROLE

2 T Butter
1 Garlic Clove, minced or 1 t powdered
1 Small Onion, sliced
1 Medium-Sized Zucchini, sliced
  Salt and Pepper, to Taste
¼ t Oregano
1 (4 oz.) Can Stewed Tomatoes
½ C Cheddar Cheese, grated

Preheat oven to 400°.

In a flameproof casserole, melt butter, saute garlic and onion for 3 minutes.

Add zucchini, salt, pepper and oregano and cook covered for 10 minutes.

Add tomatoes and place in oven for 15 minutes.

Uncover casserole, add cheese and return to oven until cheese is melted.

Serve immediately.

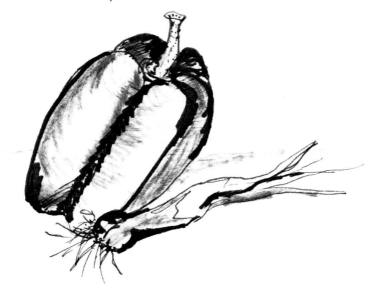

CURRIED MUSHROOMS

1/2 lb. Mushrooms, washed and sliced
4 T Butter
3/4 C Onion, minced
1 Garlic Clove, crushed or 1 t powdered
1 t Curry Powder
1/3 C Beef Broth
1/4 t Salt

Saute mushrooms and onions in butter for 5 minutes.

Add garlic and curry powder and cook 2 minutes longer or until curry powder is darkened.

Add broth and salt; reduce heat and simmer for 5 minutes.

Serves four.

IRENE COLE'S BROCCOLI

2 Pkgs. Chopped Broccoli, cooked and drained
1 T Fines Herbes
1 Can Cheddar Cheese Soup
1 Can Water Chestnuts, sliced
1 C Pepperidge Farm or Progresso Bread Crumbs
4 T Butter, melted

Alternate broccoli, chestnuts and cheddar cheese soup in two layers, adding fines herbes.

Combine bread crumbs and butter and sprinkle on top.

Bake at 350° for 20 to 30 minutes.

RATATOUILLE

1 C Onions, sliced (frozen may be used)
1 T Garlic Powder
1 C Olive Oil
2 Small Eggplants, cut into 1-inch cubes
1 Pkg. Frozen Zucchini or 4 large Zucchinis
1 Pkg. Green Peppers or 3 Green Peppers, cut into strips
2 Large Cans of Tomatoes or 1 lb. and 4 oz. Tomato Sauce
1 t Basil
1 T Salt
½ T Pepper
1 t Parsley
½ t Oregano
½ t Italian Herbs

Saute onions and garlic powder in olive oil.

Add eggplant, zucchini and peppers and saute until lightly browned.

Add tomatoes and seasonings; cover and simmer for approximately 1 hour.

Remove cover and continue cooking until most of liquid has evaporated.

Serves six.

CURRIED CORN SOUFFLE

1 package of frozen Corn Souffle (Stouffer's is best)
½t Curry Powder
2 T Butter or Margarine

Cook corn souffle according to directions. Just before serving melt the curry in the butter and either spoon on top or mix in the souffle.

Serves two.

ONION SUCCOTASH

2 boxes of frozen Succotash
1 small jar of Cocktail Onions
½t Thyme
  Salt and Pepper, to Taste

Cook the vegetables according to directions and add seasonings and onions before serving.

Serves four.

ZUCCHINI WITH APPLES

1 package of frozen, sliced Zucchini (or two pounds of fresh)
1 package of dried Apples
1 package of frozen Onions
1 large can of Tomatoes
2 sticks of Butter or Margarine
1 T Parsley
1 t Italian Herbs
Salt and Pepper, to Taste

Saute the onions, apples and zucchini in the butter. Add the tomatoes and seasoning. Simmer for about twenty minutes.

Serves six.

CREOLE GREEN BEANS

2 packages 10 oz. each of frozen Green Beans, cooked
1 t Garlic Powder
1 large can (1 pound) Tomatoes, drained
Salt and Pepper, to Taste
1 stick of Butter or Margarine
2 T chopped Onions (optional)
2 T chopped Green Pepper (optional)

Saute onions and green peppers and add to beans and tomatoes. Simmer and serve.

Serves six.

EASY MUSHROOM SPINACH

2 Pkgs. Frozen Chopped Spinach
1 Can Cream of Mushroom Soup
1 Pkg. Lipton Onion Soup Mix

Cook spinach according to directions; drain and place into a serving bowl.

Add mushroom and onion soup, stirring well.

Serves four to six.

DILLED GREEN BEANS

Canned Whole Blue Lake Green Beans
French or Italian Salad Dressing
Dill Weed
Bermuda Onions, thinly sliced (optional)

Drain beans and marinate in salad dressing.

Liberally sprinkle dill weed and mix.

If not other onions are included in the menu, Bermuda onions can be added to the marinade.

SALADS

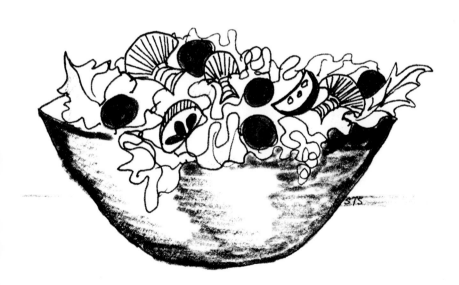

SPINACH SALAD

1 lb. Fresh Spinach

Wash spinach and remove stems. Break spinach into bite-sized pieces and chill until crisp.

Add any or all of the variations of ingredients to the spinach and toss.

VARIATIONS

1 to 2 Small Avocadoes, pitted and cubed and/or
1 Large Red Onion, thinly sliced
1 C Small Curd Cottage Cheese
1-½ C Sliced Mushrooms, fresh or canned
1 C Bacon Bits

ZIPPY SPINACH SALAD

1 (10 oz.) bag Fresh Spinach
1½ t Jane's Krazy Salt
1 t Black Pepper
2 t Dijon Mustard
2 T Red Wine Vinegar
½ C Olive Oil
¼ t Lemon Juice
1½ t Fine Herbs
8 Thinly Sliced Radishes
1 Lg. Onion, sliced in rings

Wash spinach, dry and chill.

Mix salt, pepper, mustard and vinegar.

Beat in olive oil with a fork until dressing has consistency of thin mayonnaise.

Add Fine Herbs and stir in lemon juice.

Pour over spinach, adding radishes and onions; toss and serve.

Serves four to six.

SPINACH AND ORANGE SALAD

1 Bag Spinach, washed and broken into pieces
2 Cans Mandarin Oranges, drained
  Oil and Vinegar dressing
  Worcestershire sauce

Toss spinach and oranges and serve with oil and vinegar or oil and onion dressing to which Worcestershire Sauce has been added for zest.

Serves six.

SOUR CREAM TOMATO SALAD

1 C Sliced Cucumber
3 C Tomatoes, Cut into Chunks
1 C Sliced Red Onion
1 t each Salt and Pepper
2 T Parsley
1 C Sour Cream
1 T Horseradish
2 T Vinegar (Red Wine is best)

Combine in a bowl cucumbers, tomatoes and onion.

Sprinkle over seasonings.

Pour over sour cream which has been mixed with horseradish and vinegar. Chill and serve.

Serves six.

WATERCRESS, MUSHROOM AND ENDIVE SALAD

2 C Watercress, Washed
2 C Mushrooms, Washed and Sliced
6 Heads Endive Lettuce, Washed

Use a bought Italian dressing or make a light mustard dressing using:

   2 T Tarragon Vinegar
   1 T Olive Oil
   6 T Vegetable Oil
   1 t Lemon Juice
   1 t Salt
1/2 t Freshly Ground Black Pepper
   1 t Dijon Mustard
1/8 t Sugar
      Dash — Few Drops Tabasco Sauce
      Dash — Few Drops Worcestershire Sauce
   1 Raw Egg

Beat egg well and add other ingredients.

Add dressing and toss.

Serves eight.

TREADWAY'S SALAD SURPRISE

1½ lb. Zucchini
1½ lb. Squash
 2 T Lemon Juice
 2 T Olive Oil
 3 T Salad Oil
 1 t Salt
 ½ t Dry Mustard
 ½ t Freshly Ground Pepper
 ½ t Garlic Powder

Wash and slice zucchini and squash and cook in boiling water for 5 minutes or less (it should still be crunchy).

Drain and place in a shallow dish.

To make vinaigrette, combine remaining ingredients, stirring well and pour over the squash. Marinate and serve.

Serves eight.

CUCUMBER SALAD

1 C grated Cucumber
1 pkg. Lemon Jello
2 T Vinegar
½t Salt
1 T Grated Onion
1 t Fines Herbs or dill
   Green food coloring (optional)

Dissolve the lemon jello in one cup of boiling water. Let it thicken and then add other ingredients (plus green food coloring if you desire). Place in a mold and chill.

Serve with a horseradish and mayonnaise or horseradish and sour cream sauce.

Serves four.

CUCUMBERS IN SOUR CREAM I

¾ C Sour Cream
2 T Vinegar
1 T Chives, chopped
   Salt and Pepper, to Taste
6 Medium Cucumbers, peeled and thinly sliced

Combine first four ingredients, mixing well.

Add cucumbers and chill.

CUCUMBERS IN SOUR CREAM II

4 Cucumbers, peeled and sliced paper thin
1 (8 oz.) Container Sour Cream
1 Pkg. Ranch House or other Sour Cream Seasoning or 1 t Dill
   or Tarragon and 1 t Fine Herbs

Combine chilled cucumber slices and sour cream.

Add seasonings and refrigerate until chilled.

Serves six.

ORANGE AND CUCUMBER SALAD

1 medium size Cucumber, thinly sliced
1 large can of Mandarin Oranges, drained
½C frozen Green Pepper (or two fresh peppers, chopped)
½t Salt
½t Pepper
1 T Parsley
½t Thyme
1 T Fine Herbes
½C plain Yogurt or Sour Cream

Mix and chill. Serve on crisp greens, if you desire.

Serves four.

MOLDED GAZPACHO SALAD

2 Pkgs. Unflavored Gelatin
5½ C Water
1 T Onion, grated
1 T White Wine Vinegar
1 T Olive Oil
1½ t Salt
1 (13 oz.) Can Consomme Madrilene
3 Medium Tomatoes, finely chopped
1 Medium Cucumber, peeled, seeded and finely chopped
½ Green Pepper, finely chopped
1 Small Garlic Clove, grated

On the day before party, place gelatin in a 3 qt. saucepan and add ½ C of water.

Cook over medium heat and add onion, vinegar, salt and oil.

Chill until mixture mounds slightly when dropped from a spoon.

Fold in remaining ingredients plus 4 C of water.

Chill.

Serves six.

TARRAGON SALAD WITH ARTICHOKES

1½ C Oil
1 C Tarragon Vinegar
2 t Jane's Krazy Salt
1 t Pepper
1 t Tarragon
1 t Sugar
4 Jars Marinated Artichokes
7 C Lettuce — a combination of Romaine and spinach, broken into bite size pieces
1 Bermuda Onion, Sliced or 1 bunch Scallions, Sliced
Tomatoes (optional)

Combine first six ingredients to make Tarragon Dressing.

Drain artichokes and marinate in dressing for as long as possible.

Mix marinated artichokes with dressing and lettuce, toss and serve.

Serves eight.

AVOCADO WITH BACON

4 Ripe Avocadoes
4 Lemons
4 t Crumbled Bacon (canned is fine)
4 t Capers

Slice avocadoes.

Squeeze lemon juice on them.

Sprinkle with bacon and capers.

Serves four.

EASY CAESAR SALAD

2 C Croutons (See "Easy Croutons" in Gaspacho Recipe)
   Caesar Salad Dressing
2 Large Heads of Romaine Lettuce, Chilled
   Salt and Pepper, to Taste
1 to 2 T Anchovie Paste, to Taste
1 to 2 T Garlic Powder, to Taste
1 C Parmesan Cheese, Grated

Mix seasonings in bought dressing.

Add chopped Romaine pieces.

Add cheese and toss. Add croutons.

Serves eight.

TOMATO ASPIC

2 Pkgs. Lemon Gelatin
2½ C Water
1 (12 oz.) Jar of Chilli Sauce
½ C Celery, chopped
¼ C Olives, chopped
1 t Lemon Juice

Prepare gelatin using water and blend in remainder of the ingredients.

Pour into a ring or mold and chill.

Serves eight.

BETTY LADD'S HORSERADISH MOLD

1 Pkg. Lemon or Lime Jello
½ C Boiling Water
1 Envelope Knox Gelatin
2 T Cold Water
1 Jar Hot Horseradish
1 C Mayonnaise
1 Lg. Container of Sour Cream
1 T Parsley
1 t fine herbes
Dissolve jello in boiling water.

Dissolve gelatin in cold water and add to jello.

Add all other ingredients and blend with a whisk or egg beater.

Pour mixture into a lightly-oiled mold and chill.

Serves six.

MARINATED VEGETABLE SALAD

2 C Salad Oil
1 C Vinegar
2 T Sugar
2 T Garlic Powder
   Salt and Pepper, to Taste
2 Cans of Green Beans or 3-Bean Salad
1 Can of Beets
1 C Onions, thinly sliced

Combine first five ingredients.

Place vegetables in a flat dish and pour marinade over them.

Refrigerate for at least 24 hours.

Serve chilled.

Serves ten.

RICE POTATOES & PASTA

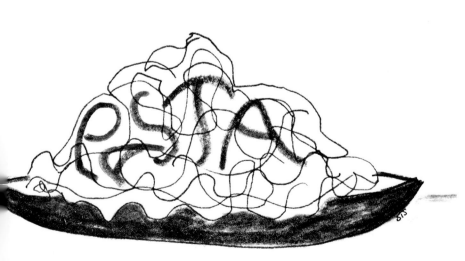

RICE WITH PINE NUTS

1 box or bag or Rice which serves 4 (seasoned is best)
1 C chopped Onions (frozen is fine)
1 C Pine Nuts
1 t Paprika
1 t Tabasco
1 stick of Butter or Margarine
1 T Parsley
2 chopped Pimientos
Salt and Pepper, to Taste

Cook the rice according to directions. Saute all the other ingredients, except the pimiento, and then add to the rice. Garnish with the pimento.

Serves six.

ORANGE RICE

1 box or bag of rice for four
1 stick of Butter
2/3 C diced Celery with leaves
3 T chopped Onion (frozen is fine)
1 small can of frozen Orange Juice, defrosted
Salt and Pepper to Taste

Melt half the butter in a saucepan and saute the celery and onion until they are tender but not brown. Add salt and pepper to taste.

Add orange juice and the water required by the recipe, minus ½ cup to make up for the juice. Add the rice and cook according to directions. Add the rest of the butter and serve with pork, chicken, or ham.

Serves six.

SUMMER RICE SALAD

3 C White cooked, steamed Rice, at room temperature
¾C of Italian or French Dressing (or more if you prefer)
1 t dry Mustard Powder
½C thinly sliced Radishes
½C thinly sliced Scallions
1 Green Pepper, minced (frozen is fine)
4 Minced Gherkin Pickles
1 small jar of Olives (optional)
½sliced Cherry Tomatoes (optional)
1 t Parsley
1 t Dill
1 t Chives
   Salt and Pepper, to Taste

Mix and serve with cold meat, poultry or fish.

Serves eight.

SPINACH RICE

1 Bag Jane's Krazy Rice Mix or other Seasoned Rice Mix
1 Box Frozen Spinach
1 C Parmesan Cheese
1 Stick Butter

Cook rice and spinach separately according to directions on package.

Just be fore serving, mix the two with the butter.

Serve the Parmesan Cheese as a topping.

Serves six to eight.

WAYS TO JAZZ UP WILD RICE

Make the rice according to directions and thoroughly drain. Then add:

Sauteed mushrooms or

Brandy or sherry or

Toasted Pine Nuts or almonds or

Sauteed onions or

Sauteed liver or

Parsley or

Sauteed celery

TONY'S WILD, WILD RICE

1 Pkg. Uncle Ben's Wild Rice, cooked as directed
1 Stick of Butter
1 Pkg. Vermicelli Noodles, broken into 1 inch pieces
½ C Slivered Almonds
2 T Chopped Green Onions or Chives
1 Lg. Can of Mushrooms, sliced and drained
3 C Chicken Broth

In a large skillet, brown the noodles in butter.

Add onions, almonds and mushrooms and continue cooking over a low flame until brown.

Add chicken broth and rice, mixing well.

Place mixture in a covered dish and bake at 325° for 1 to 1½ hours (depending on whether you enjoy moist or dry rice).

For color, serve with spiced apple rings.

Serves eight.

FRIED RICE

1 box or bag of rice that serves 4 (seasoned or brown is
  best)
1/3 C Peanut Oil
½C chopped Onions (frozen is fine)
1 C julienne strips of Smithfield Ham, or Chicken or Pork
  (or any combination of the meats)
½C Water Chestnuts
4 T Soy Sauce
1 T Parsley
  Pepper to Taste
2 Eggs

Cook the rice according to directions. Lightly saute the
onions in the oil, then the meat, and then lightly scramble
the eggs. Blend in all the other ingredients and serve.

Serves six.

JAZZED-UP RICE MIXTURES

Make your favorite rice recipe and after preparing add:

Raisins to the boiling water and then add almonds when
ready to serve the rice

Marinated Artichokes or

Chopped Celery and Water Chestnuts or

Use chicken or beef broth instead of water or

Mushrooms sauteed in butter or bacon bits and/or chopped,
sauteed onions or

Chopped walnuts, pecans, or filberts or saffron or

Parmesan cheese or

Sherry

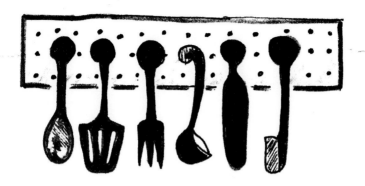

EASY STUFFED BAKED POTATOES

1 (8 oz.) Pkg. Cream Cheese or 1 Pt. Sour Cream
1 Stick Butter, softened
2 T Chives
1 T Onions, minced
1 t Paprika
6 Medium Potatoes, baked

Combine cream cheese, butter, chives, onions and paprika.

Hollow out potatoes and add to cream cheese mixture, blending well.

Stuff potatoes with mixture, sprinkling bacon bits on top for garnish and place under broiler until browned.

Serves six.

CHEESE-POTATO PUFFS

1 Pkg. Potato Pancake Mix (Panni is best) or Instant Mashed Potatoes
1 Pkg. Cheese Fondue Mix (Tiger is best)
1 Well Beaten Egg (optional)
1 t Paprika
Seasoned Bread Crumbs

Prepare potatoes according to directions, adding the egg.

Mix in the fondue and add the paprika.

Roll mixture into whatever size ball you desire and then roll in seasoned bread crumbs. Place in ice box to harden for half an hour.

Fry balls in a preheated deep fat fryer at 375° for a minute or so. Place on absorbent paper or brown bag and serve immediately.

Serves eight.

CHEESE POTATO CROWNS

3 C of cooked instant mashed potatoes
½C grated Cheddar or ¾ C Parmesan Cheese
½stick of melted Butter or Margarine
1 T Parsley
Salt and Pepper to Taste

Mix the ingredients. Arrange the mixture in eight mounds on a lightly buttered skillet or on a aluminum pan. Place under broiler for five minutes or until they are browned.

Serves four.

WAYS TO JAZZ UP FROZEN FRENCH FRIES OR HASH BROWN POTATOES

Cook according to directions and then add:

Cocktail Onions or

Shelled Pistachio nuts or

Bacon Bits or

Cooked, sliced Sausage

NANCY BRINKER'S KENNETT QUICHE

 1 Frozen Pie Shell
 1 C Bacon, cooked and crumbled
1½ C Swiss Cheese, cut into strips
 3 Eggs
 1 C Sour Cream
    Salt, Pepper and Nutmeg, to taste

Place bacon in bottom of pie shell.

Sprinkle half of cheese on top.

Place in a blender the eggs, sour cream and seasonings and blend until smooth.

Pour egg mixture into pie shell and place remainder of cheese on top.

Bake at 350º for 35 minutes.

SPICY MACARONI AND CHEESE

2 C of macaroni (eight ounces)
2 C of shredded Cheese for Tacos (if you can't find it in your supermarket, just use 1 C of sharp Cheddar Cheese and 1 C of Monterey Jack Cheese and then add ½ t Chilli Powder, ½ t Garlic Powder and ½ t Onion Powder or Flakes)
1 stick of butter or margarine
3 T Flour
1 C Heavy Cream
½C White Wine
  Salt and Pepper, to Taste

Cook the macaroni according to directions. Drain and save.

Heat the butter and stir in the flour. Slowly add the white wine and cream, and cook over a low flame, stirring constantly, until thickened.

Add the cheese and continue to stir until melted. Add salt and pepper to taste.

Mix the cheese sauce with the macaroni and simmer for another five minutes and then serve.

Serves four.

SPAGHETTI ALLA CARBONARA

1 lb. Thin Spaghetti, cooked and drained
10 Slices of Bacon, cut into julienne strips or 1 C Bacon Bits
8 T Butter
Salt, to Taste
1 C Parmesan Cheese
½ C White Wine

Toss cooked spaghetti with bacon, butter, salt, cheese and wine.

Serve immediately with remaining cheese.

Serves four.

SHRIMP MARINARA SPAGHETTI

1 large jar of Tomato Spaghetti Sauce (Ragu is best)
1 stick of Butter
1 C of chopped Onions (frozen is fine)
¼ C Olive Oil
½ T Basil
½ T Italian Herbs
1 t Garlic Powder
1 C White Wine
1 pound of shelled and cooked Shrimp
1 pound of cooked Spaghetti
Salt and Pepper to Taste

Saute the onion in the olive oil until it is golden. Add all other ingredients, except the spaghetti and butter, and simmer for about ten minutes.

Serve over the buttered spaghetti.

Serves six.

(Clams can be substituted for the shrimp)

BARLEY CASSEROLE

2 Sticks Butter
1 Large Onion, Chopped Fine
½ lb. Mushrooms, Washed
1 t Fines Herbes
   Salt and Pepper, to Taste
1 C Pearl Barley
2-3 C Boiled Chicken Broth

Using 1 stick of butter, saute the mushrooms and onion with seasonings.

Add the barley and brown it lightly.

Place mixture in well-buttered casserole or pan. Add enough broth to cover ½ inch above the mixture.

Cover and bake at 350º for 25 minutes.

Taste the barley for doneness. Add more broth and cook longer, if desired, until it is as soft as you like it.

Add the remaining butter and serve.

Serves Six.

BRIE EN CROUTE

Serve with salad course or as a luncheon main dish.

2 Pkg. Crescent Roll Mix
2 lbs. Brie Cheese
1 Egg Yolk

Wrap the triangles of the crescent rolls around the brie.

Brush egg yolk over crust.

Put in preheated oven at 425º for about 25 minutes. If crust is not brown yet, bake 5 minutes longer.

This is even better, if you cover the brie with sliced scallions before you put the crust over it.

EASY BAKED BEANS

2 Cans Baked Beans
½ lb. Bacon or ½ lb. Salt Pork (cut into 1″ squares)
2 Medium-sized Onions, sliced
2 t Salt
2 t Pepper
1 t Ground Ginger
½ C Catsup
½ C Molasses or Maple Syrup
1 T Vinegar
2 t Dried Mustard

Place all ingredients in covered pot, mixing well.

Bake at 300º for 6 to 8 hours.

They are much better the second day, so cook the evening before and then reheat.

Serves six.

JAZZED-UP STUFFING MIXTURES FOR POULTRY OR FISH

1 Pkg. Pepperidge Farm Stuffing Mix
1 Onion
6 T Butter
  Garlic Powder, to Taste
  Dash of Thyme
  Dash of Sage
  Dash of Basil
  Salt and Pepper to Taste

Saute onions in butter and add stuffing mix and seasonings. To this base add:

Sliced, dried apricots and apples or

Cooked chestnuts or salted pecan halves or toasted almonds or

Mushrooms and celery, sauteed in butter or

Mandarin oranges with or without bacon bits or

Cranberries or

Slices of sausage or

Oysters or Clams and/or spinach or

Crabmeat

SAUCE & DRESSINGS

FLOU

MUSTARD SAUCE

2½ T Olive Oil
1 T White Wine Vinegar
1 Heaping t Dijon Mustard
   Tarragon, to taste
   Salt and Pepper, to taste
   Chopped Scallions, to taste
   Dash of Worcestershire Sauce (optional)

Mix and season to taste.

This sauce is very good on steaks and salads.

MUSTARD BUTTER

1 C Butter, softened
2 T Dijon Mustard
1 t Lemon Juice
1/8 t Garlic, crushed or Garlic Powder
   Salt and Pepper, to Taste

Combine all ingredients, mixing well and mound in a shallow
dish.

Serve at room temperature.

(This is very good with lamb chops, chicken or fish.)

MUSTARD AND CHUTNEY SAUCE

1 C Dry Mustard
8 T Water
1 t Sugar
   Salt, to Taste
12 T Bottled Chutney, chopped

Combine mustard and water and stir well until smooth.

Add salt and sugar and let stand 10 minutes to develop the flavor.

Stir in chutney.

Serve as a side dish with ham or other roasts.

COLD FOOD SAUCE

1 C Marmalade
5 T Lemon Juice
3 T Orange Juice (frozen)
½t Salt
1 T Horseradish
1 t Dijon Mustard
½t Ginger
1 t fine herbes
Combine ingredients in blender.

Can be stored for weeks in ice box.

This sauce is fantastic on steak, ham, fish or meat.

HERB BUTTER FOR STEAK

2 Sticks of Butter
1 t Hickory Salt
1 t Pepper
1 t Garlic Powder
1 T Parsley
1 t Tarragon
1 t Fines Herbs
1 t Dry Mustard Powder

In a saucepan, melt butter and add ingredients, mixing well.

EASY HOLLANDAISE

½ C Butter, melted
3 Egg Yolks
2½ T Lemon Juice
  Salt, to Taste
  Cayenne Pepper, to Taste
1 T Mayonnaise

Place all ingredients in a blender and mix until blended.

WAYS TO JAZZ UP BOUGHT HOLLANDIASE

HERBED HOLLANDAISE SAUCE

1 C Hollandaise
1 t Chives
1 t Minced Shallot or Onion (optional)
1 t Parsley
¼t Tarragon
1 t Fines Herbes

Blend and serve over poultry, fish or vegetables.

DILL HOLLANDAISE SAUCE

1 C Hollandaise
1 T Dill Seed
1 T Parsley
1 T minced Onion (optional)

Blend and serve over vegetables or fish.

ORANGE HOLLANDAISE SAUCE

1 C Hollandaise
2-3 T frozen Orange Juice concentrate

Blend and serve over vegetables

SPANISH SAUCE

½C Chopped Onion (frozen is fine)
1 T Garlic Powder
1 T Butter
1 Can (1 lb.) stewed tomatoes with juice
1 t Salt
¼t Sugar
½C Coarsely chopped Green Pepper (frozen is fine)
2 T Chopped Parsley
   Hot Pepper to Taste (optional)
½C thinly sliced Celery (optional)

Saute celery, onion, and garlic in butter until onion is tender. Add tomatoes and juice, salt, sugar, simmer gently for 15 minutes. Stir in green pepper and parsley; heat.

Yield: 2¼ cups.

Serve over poultry or fish.

EASY GRAVY FOR FOWL

½C Butter
½C White Wine
½C Marmalade or Currant Jelly
1 t Garlic Powder
1 Pkg. Gravy Mix
   Salt and Pepper, to Taste

Combine all ingredients in a saucepan and heat.

In place of butter, use drippings from pan — it tastes much better.

MUSHROOM WINE SAUCE

1 Onion, finely chopped
¼ lb. Butter
1 lb. Mushrooms, thinly sliced
2 T Chopped Parsley
   Salt and Pepper, to Taste
1 t Italian Herbs
1½ C Chicken Consomme
1 C Dry White Wine
½ T Flour

Saute onions in butter.

Add mushrooms, herbs, salt and pepper and cook at low heat for 5 minutes.

Add consomme and wine.

Sprinkle in flour and let cook a few minutes to remove the flour taste.

Serve with veal, chicken or squab.

HERB BUTTER FOR SEAFOOD

2 Sticks Butter
1 t Salt
1 t Lemon Pepper
1 T Chopped Shallots
1 T Parsley
1 t Tarragon
1 t Fines Herbs

Melt butter with ingredients and mix well.

CUCUMBERS-CHIVES SAUCE FOR COLD OR HOT FISH

1 T Dijon Mustard
2 T Chives
1 C Cucumber, grated
3 T Lemon Juice
1 t Salt
1 t Pepper
1 t Fines Herbs
1 C Mayonnaise

Put all ingredients in blender and blend until smooth.

Makes 1½ cups sauce.

LEMON BUTTER FOR FISH

½C Butter
1 t Lemon Juice
1 t Vinegar
1 t Worcestershire Sauce

Melt butter in a saucepan and add other ingredients, mixing well.

Serve hot.

LAMAZE SAUCE

1 Pt. Mayonnaise
1 Pt. Chili Sauce
½C India Relish
1 Hard Boiled Egg, chopped
1 t Chopped Chives
½T Chopped Pimento
2 T Chopped Celery
1 T Prepared Mustard
  Salt and Pepper, to Taste
1 T A-1 Sauce
  Dash of Paprika

Combine all ingredients, mixing well and chill for 2 hours.

Use over cold seafood or as a salad dressing.

NINA'S WHITE SAUCE

1 stick of Butter
½pint of Whipping Cream
½C White Wine or Sherry
2-4 t Flour

Melt the butter but do not brown it. Add the cream and stir, but do not boil. Then add flour and wine slowly.

Add ½ C parsley and/or mushrooms for serving over meat or fish.

Add ½ C Parmesan Cheese to make fettachine.

Serves six as a sauce. Serves three with pasta.

HERB MARINADE FOR VEGETABLES

1 (8 oz.) bottle Italian-Style Herb and Garlic Salad Dressing
2 t Italian Herbs
1 t Dill
¼C Lemon Juice
½t Jane's Krazy Salt
2 lbs. Assorted Vegetables (carrots, cauliflower, mushrooms, broccoli, artichoke hearts, zucchini, tomatoes, etc.)

Combine all ingredients and mix well.

Arrange vegetables in shallow pan and marinate overnight in refrigerator, stirring several times.

SAUCE FOR FRESH STRAWBERRIES OR RASPBERRIES

1 part Grand Marnier Liquor
3 parts Sour Cream

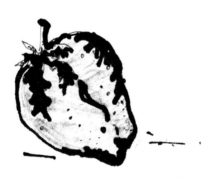

SAUCE FOR FRESH SEEDLESS GRAPES

1 part Drambuie Liquor
3 parts Sour Cream

SALAD DRESSING

3 C Oil
½C Lemon Juice
½C Vinegar
1 t Garlic Powder
½t Thyme
½t Tarragon
   Salt and Pepper, to Taste

Combine all ingredients in a jar and keep in refrigerator.

HOMEMADE MAYONNAISE

1 Egg
½t Dry Mustard
½t Salt
2 T Lemon Juice
1 C Salad Oil or (½ C Olive Oil and ½ C Peanut Oil)

Break egg into a blender and add mustard, salt, lemon juice and ¼ C of the oil and blend slowly.

When mixture is well blended, gradually add remainder of oil.

Herbs, garlic or capers can be added for variation.

GARLIC MAYONNAISE

1 C bought or homemade mayonnaise
½t dry Mustard
1 t Garlic Powder

Mix and serve on hot or cold fish, meat or vegetables.

ANCHOVY MAYONNAISE

1 to 2 T Anchovy Fillets, finely chopped
2 Garlic Cloves, crushed
¼t Parsley
¼t Basil
1 T Capers
1 T Dijon Mustard
2 C Mayonnaise

Combine all ingredients, mixing well until blended.

Serve over raw vegetables.

BACON SALAD DRESSING

3/4 lb. Bacon
2 T Bacon Drippings
1/4 C Red Wine Vinegar
3 T Tarragon Vinegar
2 Garlic Cloves, minced
2/3 C Olive Oil
1 t Worcestershire Sauce
1 t Salt
1/4 t Ground Black Pepper

Fry bacon until crisp and remove from skillet, reserving the drippings.

Crumble bacon and place in a jar with all of the ingredients, shaking well.

Chill in refrigerator.

Serves six to eight.

ANCHOVIE DRESSING

1½ C Olive Oil
1 Garlic Clove, crushed
½ C Wine Vinegar
1 Can Anchovies, chopped
Toasted Croutons

Combine garlic and oil and marinate for 2 hours in a warm place.

Combine separately the anchovies and vinegar.

Add croutons at the last minute.

FRENCH DRESSING

1/3 C Sugar
1/2 t Salt
  1 t Paprika
1/2 t Onion, grated
1/4 C Vinegar
1/3 C Catsup
1/2 C Oil

Combine all ingredients in a jar and shake well until blended.

BLEU CHEESE DRESSING

3 T Mayonnaise
3 T Bleu Cheese, crumbled
5 T Cream or Half & Half
1 T Vinegar
2 T Lemon Juice
1 t Worcestershire Sauce

Place all ingredients in a jar and shake well until blended.

LOUIS DRESSING

¾C Chili Sauce
½C Mayonnaise
2 T Minced Onion
½t Sugar
½t Worcestershire Sauce
1 T Jane's Krazy Salt
1 T Black Pepper

Combine all ingredients and mix well.

Chill and serve.

Makes 1¼ cups of dressing.

AVOCADO DRESSING

½C Oil
¼C Vinegar
1 t Jane's Krazy Salt
¼t Pepper
¼t Sugar
¼t Garlic Powder
1 Ripe Avocado, Peeled and Diced

Place all ingredients in blender and blend until smooth and creamy.

(A dash of Worcestershire Sauce can also be added for zest.)

Makes 1 cup of dressing.

DESSERTS

MRS. STEWART SAUNDERS, JR.'S
BROWN SUGAR POUND CAKE

1 lb. Light Brown Sugar
1 C White Sugar
3 Sticks of Butter
5 Eggs
3 C Flour
½t Baking Powder
½t Salt
1 T Vanilla

Combine all ingredients, mixing well.

Bake at 350º for approximately 1 hour.

SHERRY CAKE

1 Pkg. Yellow Cake Mix
1 Pkg. Instant Vanilla Pudding
4 Eggs
¾C Crisco Oil
¾C Sherry
1 t Nutmeg

Mix all ingredients well.

Pour into tube pan and bake at 350º for 45 minutes.

(Keeps for many days, remaining moist.)

ANGEL FOOD CAKE WITH HEATH BARS

1 Angel Food cake mix (Duncan Hines)
3 C of Whipping Cream or Cool Whip
1 C Confectioners Sugar (not needed if you use Cool Whip)
1 t Vanilla
6 frozen Heath Bars (they chop easier this way in a
  blender)

Cook Angel Food cake according to directions and cut off the top. Spoon out a well and save the pieces of cake.

To make the filling: Combine the whipping cream with confectioners sugar and refrigerate for 3 hours. Add the vanilla and whip the cream until it peaks. Chop the Heath bars in a blender. Add them to the whipped cream. Combine the pieces of cake with some of the mixture and fill the center hole and ice the top of the bottom half.

Place the top back on the bottom and ice the entire cake.

EASY TIPSY PARSON

1 Sara Lee Pound Cake or any Sponge Cake
1/2 C Rum
1 Container Cool Whip
1/3 C Sherry
  Maraschino Cherries or other fruit

Soak cake with rum.

Combine cool whip with sherry and spread over cake.

Top with fruit.

RHOULAC'S EASY PIE CRUST

1 Stick Butter, softened
1 Lg. Pkg. Cream Cheese, softened
1 C Flour

Combine all ingredients well and roll out to fit pie pan.

Do not bake pastry before adding filling.

Makes one layer pie crust. (9 inch)

BAKED ALASKA PIE

1 9—inch, cooked pie crust (either Rhoulac's easy recipe
  or a bought one)
1 pint each of Strawberry, Chocolate and Pistachio Ice
  Cream (or whatever flavors you desire)
3 Egg Whites
¼t Cream of Tartar
6 T Sugar
½t Vanilla
Chocolate curls or jimmies, or chopped almonds for topping
  (optional)

Soften ice cream a little. Quickly pack the pie shell with
the ice cream, alternating flavors. Freeze until firm (during
dinner or freezing ahead is best). Heat oven to 500°.

Beat cream of tartar and egg whites until foamy, adding the
sugar, a bit at a time. Beat in vanilla until the mixture is
stiff and glossy.

Heap the meringue onto the pie, spreading over all the ice
cream to the edge of the crust. Bake 3 to 5 minutes or
until top is light brown. Serve immediately.

You can garnish with chocolate curls if you desire.

Serves eight.

RUM CREAM PIE

1 Envelope Unflavored Gelatin
1/2 C Water
5 Egg Yolks
1 C Sugar
1/3 C Dark Rum
1/2 C Whipping Cream
1 Baked Crumb Pie Crust
Unsweetened Chocolate, grated

Place water and gelatin in a saucepan over low heat to dissolve.

Beat egg yolks and sugar in a bowl until light.

Stir gelatin into eggs; cool, and gradually add rum, beating constantly.

Whip cream separately and fold into mixture.

Cool until mixture begins to set, then spoon into crust.

Grate chocolate on top.

RUM OR BOURBON APPLE PIE

1/3 C Bourbon or Rum
2 Jars Apple Filling
1 Pie Crust (9 inch)

Combine ingredients and pour into pie crust.

Bake at 325º for about 50 minutes or until crust is golden brown.

BRANDY, RUM (OR BOTH) MINCE PIE

1/3 C Brandy, Rum or Both
1 Lg. Jar Minced Meat
1 Pie Crust (9 inch)

Combine minced meat with liquor and pour into pie crust.

Bake at 350º for about 50 minutes or until crust is golden brown.

PEANUT BUTTER PIE

4 oz. Cream Cheese
1 C Sugar
1/3 C Peanut Butter
1/2 C Milk
1 (9 oz.) Pkg. Non-Dairy Whipped Topping
1 9-inch Graham Cracker Crust or baked Pie Crust
1/4 C Peanuts, finely chopped

Whip cheese until soft and fluffy.

Beat in sugar and peanut butter.

Slowly add milk and blend well.

Fold topping into mixture and pour into pie shell, sprinkling peanuts on top.

Freeze until firm and serve.

If not used the same day, wrap pie in plastic wrap after pie is frozen.

STRAWBERRY-RHUBARB PIE

1 (16 oz.) Pkg. Frozen Rhubarb, thawed
1 (10 oz.) Pkg. Frozen Strawberries, thawed
½ C Cointreau
¼ C Sugar
2 t Cinnamon
   Pie Crust (either purchased or recipe with cream cheese, flour
   and butter)

Mix all ingredients well and pour into pie crust.

Bake at 450° for about 30 minutes.

BLUEBERRY REFRIGERATOR PIE

1 Pkg. Cream Cheese
1 C Powdered Sugar
1 t Vanilla
1 Pt. Whipping Cream
2 Baked Pie Shells
2 T Lemon Juice
1 Can Blueberry Pie Filling

Beat cream cheese, sugar and vanilla until well blended.

Whip cream and fold into cream cheese mixture, then pour into
2 baked pie shells; refrigerate until set.

Add lemon juice to pie filling and spread on top.

Refrigerate at least several hours before serving.

SOUR CREAM BLUEBERRY PIE

¼ lb. Cream Cheese
2 C Sour Cream
½ C Sugar
1 Graham Cracker Crumb Pie Shell
1½ C Blueberries (frozen are fine but then leave out some of the sugar required)
½ t Nutmeg
½ t Cinnamon

Combine cream cheese, sour cream and sugar, and pour into pie shell.

Spoon blueberries evenly on top.

Sprinkle nutmeg, cinnamon and extra sugar (usually 1 T) on top.

Bake at 350º for 5 minutes, then chill and serve.

Serves six.

CHESS PIE

½C Butter
1 C Brown Sugar
1 C White Sugar
3 Eggs, beaten
1 t Vanilla
1 Uncooked Pastry Shell

Melt butter in a saucepan.

Add sugars and beaten eggs and vanilla.

Pour into pie shell and bake at 350º until filling sets.

QUICK MOUSSE

1 (6 oz.) Pkg. Chocolate Bits
2 Eggs
3 T Strong Coffee
2 T Rum or Grand Marnier
¾C Scalded Milk

Combine all ingredients in blender and blend at high speed.

Pour into glasses and chill.

Serves four to six.

MAPLE SYRUP MOUSSE

1 C Maple Syrup, Chilled
2 Lg. Containers Cool Whip
  Macaroons

Mix first two ingredients well and place in parfait glasses putting macaroon on top of each.

Chill in refrigerator or place glasses in freezer for ½ hour or if using plastic, freeze for 1 hour before serving to make a frozen mousse, which is even tastier.

Serves Six.

COFFEE MOUSSE

1/3 C Confectioners Sugar
2 Eggs
1/4 C Instant Coffee
1 Pint Whipping Cream (or Cool Whip for dieters)
1 T Meyers Rum or Tia Maria

Combine sugar and egg whites and beat until frothy.

Add whipped cream or Cool Whip and beat until stiff.

Add egg yolks, coffee and rum. Mix.

Freeze in pie plate covered with Saran Wrap to avoid crystals.

BAKED PEARS OR PEACHES

6 Ripe Pears or Peaches (canned may be used)
2¼ C Port
½ C Crumbled Macaroons
¼ C Finely Chopped Pecans
1 T Grated Lemon Rind
6 T Butter (optional)

Peel, core and slice fruit and arrange in an oven-proof dish.

Combine in a bowl port, macaroons, pecans, lemon rind and butter.

Mix well and fill fruit halves.

Pour 1 cup port around pears and bake at 350º for 20 minutes.

Remove from oven and broil for a few minutes until fruit is tender when pierced with a knife.

Makes twelve fruit halves.

STRAWBERRIES CORDIAL

3 Pkgs. Frozen Strawberries, Thawed
3 Pkgs. Frozen Raspberries, Thawed
1/2 C Kirsch
1/3 C Sugar (brown sugar has a different sensation)
1 C Whipped Cream or Cool Whip

Puree raspberries, kirsch and sugar in blender.

Pour over strawberries, cover and chill.

Serve with whipped cream, if desired.

Serves Six.

STRAWBERRIES TSARINA

2 C Fresh Strawberries, washed and hulled
2 T Port
2 T Orange Curacao
2 T Cognac
  Powdered Sugar, to Taste

Combine liquors and sugar and marinate strawberries 1 hour before serving.

Serve with whipped cream or additional Curacao on top.

STRAWBERRIES ROMANOFF

1 Qt. Vanilla Ice Cream, softened
½ Pt. Heavy Cream, whipped
½ C Cointreau
   Juice of 1 Lemon
1 Qt. Fresh Strawberries, washed and capped
2 T Sugar

Beat ice cream, heavy cream, ¼ cup Cointreau and lemon juice together, put in freezer; stir often so that it does not get too hard.

Sprinkle strawberries with sugar and remainder of Cointreau and put in freezer for a short while.

Before serving ice cream, add strawberries.

RASPBERRY GINGER

3 (10 oz.) Pkgs. of Frozen Raspberries
1½ Pints Heavy Cream (or Cool Whip for dieters)
1 C Sifted Light Brown Sugar (or if using Cool Whip, ½ C)
½ t Ginger

Thaw raspberries and drain thoroughly. Gently separate berries.

Whip cream until stiff.

Mix brown sugar with ginger and fold into the cream.

Fold raspberries in gently, so as not to crush them.

Chill for at least one hour or so until ready to serve.

Before serving, stir gently to blend in any juices.

Serves four.

APPLESAUCE BRULE

1 Jar Prepared Applesauce
Cinnamon, to Taste
Raisins, to Taste
Brown Sugar, to Taste
Lemon Juice, to Taste

Add cinnamon and raisins to applesauce.

Chill well.

Cover with brown sugar and lemon juice and place under broiler until bubbly.

CREME DE CACAO CHANTILLY

2 T Gelatin
½C Cold Water
2 C Strong Coffee
¾C Creme De Cacao
3 t Sugar
2 Pts. Whipped Cream, flavored with Creme de Cacao

Soften gelatin in cold water and add hot coffee to dissolve.

Add Creme de Cacao and sugar and stir until dissolved.

Pour into ring mold and refrigerate.

Before serving, fill center of ring with whipped cream and grate chocolate over the cream.

CURRIED FRUIT

1 Can Pear Halves
1 Can Peaches or Apricots
1 Can PIneapple Slices
  Prunes (optional)
1/3 C Butter
3/4 C Brown Sugar
  4 t Curry Powder

Drain and dry fruit.

Melt butter, sugar and curry powder in a saucepan.

Place fuit and butter mixture in a 1½ quart casserole and bake at 325° for 1 hour.

Serve warm with lamb or poultry.

If you substitute brandy for the curry and serve with whipped cream, it can be served for dessert.

Serves twelve.

CHEESE WITH FRUIT

Cheese	Fruit	Wine (optional)
Brie	Pears	Port
Camembert	Strawberries or Oranges	Tokay or Champagne
Gourmandise	Cherries	
Liederkranz	Bananas	
Bel Paise	Nuts	Sherry
Port du Salut	Apples	Madeira
Roquefort	Pears or Tokay Grapes	Port
Edam, Gouda	Green Grapes or Apples	
Fontina	Figs or Dates	
Gruyere	Pineapple	
Swiss	Melons	

CANTALOUPE IN PORT

2 Lg. Cantaloupes
1½ C Port
   Juice of 1 Lemon

Shape cantaloupes into balls.

Place melon balls in a bowl and add port and lemon juice.

Marinate for 2 or 3 hours in the refrigerator.

Serve chilled with fresh mint.

Serves five or six.

POTS DE CREME AU CHOCOLAT

3 Square Unsweetened Chocolate
1 t Water
3 T Sugar
3 C Light Cream
6 Egg Yolks
1 t Vanilla

Melt chocolate and water in saucepan over very low heat, stirring with wooden spatula.

Combine sugar and cream in a bowl and beat.

Pour chocolate into cream and stir well.

Beat egg yolks in a separate bowl and slowly add chocolate mixture.

Add vanilla and pour through a fine strainer into 8 pot de creme containers.

Place containers in a pan of warm water and bake at 325° for 25 minutes until barely set.

Serves eight.

EASY BLUEBERRY PARFAIT

1 (10 oz.) Pkg. Frozen Blueberries
½C Cointreau or Grand Marnier
1 Pint LIme Sherbert

Thaw blueberries and mix with liquor.

Serve over lime sherbert.

Serves six.

APPLESAUCE BROWNIES

½C Butter
2 oz. Unsweetened Chocolate
1 C Sugar
2 Eggs, well beaten
½C Applesauce
1 t Vanilla
1 C Flour
½t Baking Powder
¼t Baking Soda
¼t Salt
½C Chopped nuts (optional)

Preheat oven to 375⁰.

Melt butter and chocolate in a double boiler.

Remove chocolate from heat and stir in remaining ingredients.

Pour mixture into an 8-inch square pan and bake for 35 to 40 minutes.

MACAROON DESSERT

18 Macaroons, broken into pieces
1 Pt. Whipping Cream or Cool Whip
1 t Vanilla
1 t Sugar
1 C Chopped Walnuts
1 Pt. Lemon or Lime Sherbert
1 Pt. Raspberry Sherbert
   Pinch of Salt

Whip cream and add macaroons, walnuts, vanilla, sugar and salt.

Spread mixture on a 9" x 13" pan.

Spoon sherbert on top, alternating the colors.

Spread some of macaroon mixture on top.

Freeze.

Serves ten to twelve.

EASY CHOCOLATE BROWNIE

2 Sticks Butter
7 Squares Chocolate
1 C Flour
2 C Sugar
7 Eggs
   Pinch of Salt
2 t Vanilla

Melt butter and chocolate in a saucepan.

Remove chocolate from heat and add flour, sugar, eggs, salt and vanilla, beating well.

Grease and line pans with waxed paper or flour and pour in mixture.

Bake at 350° for 30 to 45 minutes.

BETSY KLEEBLATT'S CHOCOLATE DELIGHT

6 oz. Chocolate Bits
¾C Scalded Milk
2 Eggs
3 T Strong Hot Coffee
2 T Dark Rum
½C Chopped Walnuts
   Whipped Cream or Coffee Ice Cream

Combine in blender the chocolate bits, milk, eggs, coffee and rum.

Blend at high speed for 1½ minutes.

Add walnuts and blend 30 seconds longer.

Pour mixture into six ramekins and refrigerate overnight.

When ready to serve, top with ice cream and/or whipped cream.

Serves six.

MERINGUE SHELLS

4 Egg Whites, whipped
1 C Brown Sugar
1 C White Sugar
   Vanilla, to Taste

Combine all ingredients and form shells on greased flat pan.

Bake at 250⁰ for 1 hour. Leave in another hour with the oven off.

MRS. STEWART SAUNDER'S PUDDING

2/3 C Milk
  2 Egg Yolks
  1 C Sugar
  1 T Gelatin, softened in 1/3 C Milk
  Pinch of Salt
  2 Egg Whites
  1 C Whipped Cream
  1 T Vanilla

In a saucepan, add 2/3 C of milk, egg yolks, sugar, gelatin and salt; beat well.

Heat mixture gently to dissolve sugar, stirring constantly.

Pour mixture into mold and place mold in pan containing 1 inch of water.

Bake at 350° for 1 hour or until a knife when inserted in center, comes out clean. Cool custard.

Beat egg whites until foamy and fold in whipped cream and vanilla, and continue beating until a thick meringue is formed.

Spoon meringue on top of custard and place in refrigerator.

CREAM BRULEE

1 Qt. Heavy Cream
1 Vanilla Bean
10 Egg Yolks
1/3 C Brown Sugar

Put cream in a double boiler and heat to boiling point, infusing it with vanilla bean.

In a separate bowl, beat sugar and egg yolks.

Remove vanilla bean from cream and add cream slowly to egg mixture. Return to double boiler and heat, stirring constantly.

When spoon is coated, place mixture in a heat-proof serving dish.

Chill custard well and before serving, top with sieved brown sugar and place under broiler until sugar is glazed.

Serve as is or with fresh or frozen raspberries or strawberries.

You may also sprinkle 2 T Cointreau on top and ignite.

IRISH COFFEE ICE CREAM

1 Pint Coffee Ice Cream
3 T Instant Expresso Coffee
3 T Irish Whiskey or Bourbon
1 C Whipped Cream (or Cool Whip)

Let ice cream soften.

Dissolve coffee in whiskey.

Stir whiskey mixture into ice cream.

Refreeze in ice tray.

Serve topped with whipped cream (and chocolate bits, if you desire).

OTHER DELIGHTFUL ICE CREAMS

Strawberry Ice Cream mixed with Kirsch.

Raspberry Ice Cream mixed with Drambuie.

Peach Ice Cream mixed with Noyal de Poissy.

Chocolate Ice Cream mixed with Cointreau.

MOCHA SUNDAE

Coffee Ice Cream
Kalua or any coffee liqueur
Shaved Chocolate, to garnish

Coffee ice cream and Kalua is also good with macaroon bits or nougat bits.

CHOCOLATE NUT SAUCE FOR ICE CREAM

1 (6 oz.) Pkg. Chocolate Bits, melted
¼ lb. Butter
½ C Toasted Walnut Bits

Heat all ingredients in a saucepan and serve over ice cream — gets very hard.

CHOCOLATE MINT SAUCE FOR ICE CREAM

¼ C Water
¼ C Strong Black Coffee
¼ C Sugar
3½ Squares Semi-Sweet Chocolate, grated
1 Square Unsweetened Chocolate, grated
2 T Mint Flavored Liquer
2 T Brandy
1 t Butter

Heat first five ingredients in a saucepan over moderate heat and stir in the last three ingredients.

Serve over vanilla ice cream.

FUDGE SAUCE FOR ICE CREAM

½ C Cocoa
1 C Sugar
1 C Light Karo Syrup
Pinch of Salt
3 T Butter
1 t Vanilla
Tia Maria, to Taste

Combine all ingredients in a saucepan and heat until blended.

Serve over ice cream.

SNACKS BREADS & BARBECUES

GRILLED CHEESE, BACON AND FRUIT SANDWICH

2 Slices Bread
2 Slices American Cheese
4 Slices Bacon, cooked
   Apple Slices, Pineapple Slices or chutney
   Butter

Lightly butter outside of bread slices.

Between bread, place cheese, bacon and fruit.

Grill sandwich until cheese melts and outside of bread is toasted.

GRILLED OR COLD CHEESE SANDWICH

   Rye or White Bread Slices
   Swiss Cheese Slices or other Mild Cheese
½C Butter, Softened
1 T Minced Chutney
1 to 2 t Dijon Mustard
1 t Worcestershire Sauce
   Radish Rose and Pickle for Garnish

To make chutney mustard butter:
Combine in a bowl, softened butter, chutney, Dijon mustard and Worcestershire Sauce and stir.

Spread slices of bread with butter mixture and add cheese.

Add lettuce, if served cold. Grilled ham or bacon is good hot or cold.

Garnish with radish rose and pickle.

OPEN-FACED CHEESE AND MUSHROOM SANDWICHES

4 English Muffins, sliced and buttered
8 Thin Slices of Ham or Canadian Bacon
2 lbs. Mushrooms, sauteed
1 t Garlic Powder
   Salt and Pepper, to Taste
1 Pkg. Cheese Fondue Mix or 1 C Parmesan and/or Gruyere Cheese

Half cook bacon/ham and muffins.

Place bacon/ham on muffin.

Saute mushrooms and season with herbs, placing mushroom on top of meat.

Place cheese on top of mushrooms and put in broiler for 2 to 3 minutes or until cheese is melted and lightly browned.

Serves seven to eight.

BOURSINBURGER

Ground Beef for Patty
Boursin Cheese
Salt and Pepper, to Taste

Season beef with salt and pepper to taste.

Place 1 heaping T Boursin Cheese in middle of patty.

Brie or Blue Cheese is also good.

ZIPPY PARTY OR PICNIC SUBMARINE SANDWICHES

1 Lg. Loaf Fresh Bread
1 Stick Butter, softened
1 T Olive Oil
1 T White Wine Vinegar
½t Garlic Powder
  Salt and Pepper, to Taste
1 Small Head of Lettuce, separated
½lb. Salami, sliced
2 Tomatoes, sliced
6 oz. Swiss Cheese, sliced
½lb. Boiled Ham, sliced
1 Cucumber, thinly sliced
1 Lg. Onion, sliced
3 T Dijon Mustard (optional)
1 T Hot Peppers (optional)
2 T Chutney

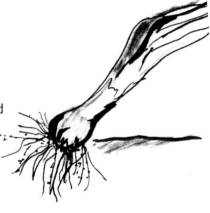

Halve bread horizontally and spread both halves with butter.

Mix oil, vinegar, garlic, salt, pepper, mustard and hot peppers.

Dip lettuce leaves into mixture.

Layer all other ingredients on bread and secure with toothpicks.

Serves six.

(May also be placed in foil and heated at 300° for 15 minutes for hot sandwiches.)

EASY PIZZA

1 Can Tomato Paste
2 English Muffins, Broken evenly in half
1 C Parmesan or Mozzerella Cheese, Grated
   Italian Seasoning, to Taste

Toast muffins on flat sides only at least 5 inches below broiled heat.

On broken sides spread:
Tomato paste and adding Italian Seasoning to taste. Place cheese on top.

Bacon, anchovies, mushrooms or other toppings may be placed on top of cheese.

Return to broiler and toast until the cheese is thoroughly melted.

JAZZED UP ROAST BEEF SANDWICHES

   Cooked Roast Beef, Sliced Thin
   Pumpernickel or White Bread Slices
½C Butter, Softened
¼C Fresh Horseradish, Finely Grated
   Salt and Cayenne, to Taste
   Parsley for Garnish
   Chutney (optional)
To make horseradish butter, combine in a bowl, softened butter, horseradish, salt and cayenne to taste, and stir.

Spread horseradish butter on slices of bread, add roast beef and parsley to garnish.

CANADIAN BACON AU GRATIN

1 C Heavy Cream
1 lb. Cheddar Cheese, diced
1 T Worcestershire Sauce
1 t Fine Herbs
1 t Dijon Mustard
  Juice of 1 Lemon
  Salt and Pepper, to Taste
1 Pkg. Canadian Bacon (about 10 slices)
1 C Mushrooms, sliced
1 Pkg. English Muffins

Heat cream in a double boiler and add cheese and seasonings, stirring well until smooth.

Gradually add lemon juice.

Brown bacon and place on muffins, pouring cream mixture on top in a flat pan.

Bake at 350⁰ for 30 minutes.

BEVERLY HATA'S CHEESE-TOPPED FRENCH BREAD

2 C Soft Sharp Cheese, grated if necessary
½t Salt
  Few Grains of Cayenne
1 t Prepared Mustard
3 T Cream or 1 to 2 T Soft Butter

Combine and stir to a smooth paste or blend in an electric blender all of the above ingredients.

Spread mixture on 1-inch slices of French Bread and place in a 350⁰ oven or under the broiler until lightly browned.

This spread is quick to make and may be kept in a closed jar in the refrigerator for weeks.

GARLIC BREAD

1 Loaf French Bread
1½ Sticks Butter, Melted
1 T Garlic Powder
1 t Parsley

Slice bread. Combine butter with garlic and parsley and brush on bread.

Place bread in foil and bake at 400° for about 15 minutes.

Serves six.

HERB BREAD

Add 2 T Fines Herbs to butter mixture.

BLEU CHEESE BREAD

Add ¼ C softened Bleu Cheese to mixture.

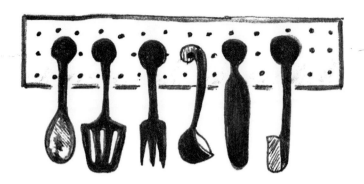

OUTDOOR GRILL

Put fresh or canned mushrooms on a strip of aluminum foil. Add salt, pepper, fine herbs and butter. Fold up foil and cook mushrooms over medium heat for about 10 minutes — 5 minutes each side.

Put washed and hulled corn cob on strip of aluminum foil. Add salt, pepper and melted butter. Fold up foil and cook over medium heat for about 10 minutes — 5 minutes each side.

Put a skinned banana on strip of aluminum foil. Add melted butter and brown sugar. Wrap and cook over medium heat 5 to 8 minutes.

Peel and core an apple. Place a mixture of soft butter, brown sugar and raisins in the middle and roll up foil. Cook for 10 minutes over medium heat — 5 minutes each side.

Cut 4 medium Zucchini Squash diagonally in ¼ inch slices. Slice 3 small tomatoes into thin wedges. Add 3 T thinly sliced green onions. Layer vegetables on doubled 18-inch aluminum foil. Dot each layer with parmesan cheese and butter. Wrap foil securely, but not tightly. Grill about 30 minutes, 4 to 6 inches from heat, turning two or three times.

BARBECUE HINTS

Put vegetables and meat on separate skewers, cooking meat longer.

Butter ½ inch slices of French Bread on both sides. Grill each side for a minute or two or until golden brown and you have a delightful addition to any barbecue.

EASY MARINADE FOR LAMB, CHICKEN OR FISH KABOBS

1/2 C Salad Oil
1/3 C Lemon Juice
　1 T Garlic Powder
　2 t Salt
　1 T Dill Weed
　1 t Pepper

Combine all ingredients and mix well.

Makes four servings.

BARBECUE SAUCE FOR RIBS OR CHICKEN

¼ C Butter
½ C Catsup
½ C Orange Juice
½ C Honey
¼ C Lemon Juice
2 T Soy Sauce
½ t Ginger

Melt all ingredients in sauce pan.

Makes two cups.

BARBECUE SAUCE FOR CHICKEN, HAMBURGER OR CHOPS

4 C Soy Sauce
1 C Bourbon
3 to 4 t Ginger
½ t Garlic, Grated
2 T Sugar
1 T fine herbes
Melt all ingredients in sauce pan.

It can be stored in ice box for weeks.

Makes five cups.

BEVERAGES

SIMPLE IRISH COFFEE (OR SANKA)

1½ oz. Irish Whiskey
1-1½ t Sugar (brown sgar may be used)
½ C Strong Black Coffee or Sanka (or less depending on glass size)
2 T Whipped Cream or Cool Whip (for dieters and people in a hurry)

In a glass, mix the sugar and whiskey (Also, if using instant coffee or Sanka; add now.)

Add hot coffee or water, stirring.

Add Cool Whip.

(A dash of Kalua and/or Creme de Menthe can be dribbled on top of cream.)

Serves one.

MORE COMPLICATED IRISH COFFEE (OR SANKA)

½ Lemon
1-1½ t Sugar (brown sugar may be used)
2 oz. Irish Whiskey
½C Strong Black Coffee or Sanka (or less depending on glass size)
½ oz. Kalua
2 T Whipped Cream or Cool Whip (for dieters or people in a hurry)
Dash of Creme de Menthe

Rub the lemon around the glass.

Place sugar in a dish and dip the glass into it to coat the rim.

Heat the glass over a flame.

Dip glass in whiskey and then take it out and ignite it, letting it burn until the flame extinguishes.

Mix in a separate container the coffee, whiskey and Kalua.

Pour coffee into glasses and add cream.

Pour Creme de Menthe on top.

Serves one.

SASSAFRAS COCKTAIL

1 Can Daiquiri or Lemonade Mix
Rum, Vodka or Gin
Fresh Mint
Soda Water

Using Daiquiri Mix can as a measuring instrument, put in blender 1 can of liquor, ¾ can of fresh mint and Daiquiri Mix and blend well.

Add 2 cans of soda water and serve.
Serves four.

EASY PLANTERS PUNCH

1 Can Frozen Tangerine or Orange Juice
2 Cans Soda Water
1 Can Meyers Rum or Light Rum, if you prefer
Dash of Bitters

Place juice in blender.

Using juice can to measure, add rum, and mix.

Add soda water and serve with a dash of bitters.
Serves four.

FISH HOUSE PUNCH

1½ C Sugar
1 Qt. Fresh Lime or Lemon Juice
2 Qts. 80-Proof Light Rum
2 Qts. Cold Water
4 oz. Peach Brandy
1 Qt. Cognac

Place sugar and lime juice in a two-gallon punch bowl and stir until sugar is thoroughly dissolved.

Stir in rum, water, peach brandy and cognac.

Allow punch to ripen at room temperature for at least three hours, stirring occasionally.

When ready to serve, place a block of ice in bowl.

Makes 1½ gallons punch.

EASY EGGNOG

1 Qt. Ready-Made Eggnog
½ Bottle Rum, Brandy or Whiskey
  Nutmeg, to Taste
  Cinnamon, to Taste

Combine first two ingredients.

Sprinkle nutmeg and cinnamon on top when ready to serve.

EASY THICK EGGNOG

1 Qt. Ready-Made Eggnog
½ Bottle Rum, Brandy or Whiskey
½ Pt. Vanilla or Eggnog Ice Cream
  Nutmeg, to Taste
  Cinnamon, to Taste

Combine first three ingredients.

Sprinkle nutmeg and cinnamon on top when ready to serve.

PUERTO RICAN RUM PUNCH

½ Shot Triple Sec
1 Shot Cherry Herring
1 Shot Rum (Moutegay is best)
½ C Pineapple Juice

Put all ingredients into shaker with ice and shake well.

Pour into glass.

Makes one glass.

SYLLABUB

1 T Sugar
4 T White Wine
  Grated Rind and Juice of 1 Lemon
  Dash of Brandy
¼ Pt. Whipped Cream

Pour first four ingredients into jug and leave for ½ hour while sugar dissolves.

Add whipped cream and serve in wine glasses.

Serves four.

EASY SANGRIA

1 Bottle Mateus Rose Wine
1½ (10 oz.) Bottle Soda Water
1 Small Can Frozen Orange Juice
1 Small Can Frozen Lemon Juice
1 Sliced Orange
  (½ Can Brandy or Port, optional.)

Mix all ingredients and serve.

Makes one large pitcher.

CAROLINA SANGRIA

8 T Sugar
1 C Orange Juice
3/4 C Lemon Juice
1 Bottle Red Wine
1/2 C Cognac
1/2 C Rum
2/3 bottle or 1 C of Soda Water

Mix well all ingredients, except the soda water which should only be added when ready to serve.

Garnish with fresh fruits.

Serves four.

EASY MINT JULEPS

2 C Bourbon
2 C Soda Water
½C Honey
½C Fresh Mint

Combine all ingredients and store in refrigerator for use.

EASY MINT TEA

8 Boston Mint-in-Tea Bags or Regular Tea
6 Sprigs Fresh Mint
4 T Sugar, if desired
2 (6 oz.) Cans Frozen Lemonade

Seep tea by pouring boiling water over tea and half of mint leaves.

Add sugar.

Let seep and pour into gallon container.

Add lemonade and fill container with water and add remaining mint.

BANANA DAIQUIRI

1 Can Frozen Daiquiri Mix
2 Bananas
1-2 Cans of Rum

Using Daiquiri can as a measuring instrument, measure rum, Daiquiri mix and bananas into a blender.

Blend well and serve.

(Peaches and strawberries are also good.)

SCORPIONS

1 oz. Brandy
1 oz. Light Rum
2½ oz. Orange Juice
½ oz. Orange Curacao
½ oz. Orange Syrup
1 Spear Fresh Pineapple
  Shaved ice.

Combine all ingredients and shake with ice.

Serve with pineapple spear.

Makes one large drink.

SOME INEXPENSIVE BUT GOOD QUALITY WINES

Red

Pasqua Valpolicella
Rene Barbier Red
Beaujolais Superior Latour
Louis Latour
Mondavi Burgundy (½ gallon)
Chantefleur by Thomas-Basset
Lamont Burgundy (½ gallon)

Rosé

Canalinno Rosé from Portugal
Tavel la Marcelle Chapoutier

White

Lamont Chablis (½ gallon)
Pasqua Soave
Rene Barbier
Mondavi Chablis (½ gallon)
Chantefleur by Thomas-Bassot

Cooking Sherry

Lamont Sherry

Cooking Brandy

Leroux Brandy

BALI PUNCH

2 ounces Rum (dark)
1 ounce Orange Juice
1 ounce Pineapple Juice
½ounce Lemon
½ounce Grenadine

CHINA SPECIAL

½ounce Brandy
1 ounce Green Creme de Menthe
½ounce Countreau
½ounce Cream

Blend and serve with dash of nutmeg or cherry (optional).

HANGOVER BREAKFAST

1 large can of Tomato Juice
2 T Worchestershire Sauce
2 T Real Lemon Juice
  Salt and Pepper, to Taste

Shake and serve very cold.

This drink, combined with strawberry or blueberry crepes
(easily made by just thinning out a packaged pancake mix)
or an omelet or scrambled eggs filled with develed ham and
sauteed mushrooms, will put you on the road to recovery.

SUGGESTED MENUS & STAPLES

SUGGESTED MENUS

Any of these recipes can be combined with others, these are just suggestions. Don't forget that sauces can jazz up any meal, especially if you are really short of time and cannot prepare full menus.

VARIOUS DINNER MENUS

Easy Clam Chowder
Orange Chicken
Mushrooms and Spinach
Strawberries Romanoff

Spinach Soup
Garlic Tails
Ratatouille
Salad
Blueberry Pie

Zucchini Soup
Steak and Lobster Kabobs
Rice with Almonds and Raisins
Salad Greens with Mustard Dressing
Maple Syrup Mousse

Onion Soup
Veal Veronique
Zucchini Casserole
Betsy's Chocolate Delight

Cream of Crab Soup
Maude's Steak
Tony's Noodles
Salad
French Bread
Fresh Fruit and Cheese (pears with
blue cheese or Brie with oranges
or cheddar with apples)

Asparagus Soup
Filet of Sole
Spinach and Mushroom Souffle
Baked Potato
Ice Cream with Fudge Sauce

ENGLISH DINNER

Potted Shrimp
Poached Salmon
Tomato, Cucumber and
Sour Cream Salad
Raspberry Ginger

FRENCH DINNER

Crabmeat Stuffed Artichokes
Surprise Chicken
Barley
Artichokes and Peas
Chocolate Mousse

ITALIAN DINNERS

Stuffed Parmesan Mushrooms
Lemon Veal
Spinach Rice
Cantaloupe in Port

Spaghetti Carbonara
Lemon Chicken with Mushrooms
Jazzed Up Green Beans
Spinach Salad
Baked Pear or Peach

MEXICAN DINNER

Guacamole
Chili Mio
Green Salad
Cheese Bread
Blueberry Parfait

EASY LUNCHES

Curried Crabmeat Salad or
Brie en Croute or
Spiced Shrimp
With Easy Curry Soup first and
Mousse for dessert

EASY LATE-NIGHT DINNERS

Quiche
Watercress, Endive and
Mushroom Salad
Herb Bread
Tipsy Parson

Swiss Chicken
Broccoli
Tipsy Parson or
Ice Cream with Fudge Sauce

EASY DINNER FOR TWO

Steak Schiffer
Broiled Tomatoes
Salad with Brie and French Bread
or Brie en Croute
Ice Cream with Liqueur

SUMMER COLD DINNER

Prosciutto and Melon
Tony's Chicken Salad
Marinated vegetables
Brownies

BARBECUE

Cold Curried Peas, Broccoli or
Spinach Soup
Steak, Chicken, Hamburgers,
Ribs, etc.
Corn on the Cob
Mushrooms or Zucchini
Bread
Bananas or Apples

SUMMER COCKTAIL PARTY

New Potatoes with Caviar or Chives
Pickled Mushrooms
Raw Vegetables with any of the dips
Raw Mushrooms Stuffed with
Boursin Cheese or Pate
Bacon Crisps
Cheese Ball
Seafood Mousse
Pate
Spiced or Curried Nuts

WINTER COCKTAIL PARTY

Caviar and Egg
Peanut Surprises
Swedish Meatballs
Canned Artichokes, Green
Beans, Onions, Beets, etc. or
Raw Vegetables and
any of the Dips
Mushrooms Stuffed with
Crabmeat or
Parmesan Cheese
Pate
Nina's Sinful Canapes
Cheese Ball
Spiced or Curried Nuts

USEFUL INGREDIENTS TO ALWAYS HAVE
IN YOUR KITCHENS FOR EASY MEALS

REFRIGERATOR/FREEZER STORAGE

Cold Food Sauce
Bourbon Barbecue
Butter
Sour Cream
Frozen Chicken Breasts
Frozen Spinach Souffle
Broccoli Au Gratin
Frozen Peas

Frozen Avocado Mix
Cream Cheese
Frozen Onions
Frozen Green Peppers
Lemon Juice
Pate
Frozen Shrimp
Frozen Hamburger
Cool Whip

CABINET STORAGE

Wines
Sherry
Dry Vermouth
Dijon Mustard
Asparagus Spears
Whole Blue Lake Green Beans
Marinated Artichokes
Canned Mushrooms
Peanut Butter
Chutney
Canned Tomatoes
Pea and Cheese Soups
Beef and Chicken Bouillon
Mandarin Oranges
Oil
Soy Sauce

Canned Crabmeat
Canned Artichoke Hearts
Caviar
Krazy Jane Salt
Krazy Jane Pepper
Lemon Pepper
Curry Powder
Fines Herbs
Italian Herbs
Garlic Powder
Bacon Bits (real not dried)
Dried Onion Soup
Chives
Ginger
Packaged Dressings
Cocktail Pastry Shells
Seasoned Rice

MAKING IT: IN LESS THAN AN HOUR

Schiffer Publishing, Ltd.
Box E, Exton, Pa. 19341

Please send me_____ copies of your cookbook at $8.95 each postage included. I enclose $8.95 per copy, a total of $_____ .
Penna. residents, please add $ .54 tax, for each copy.

NAME_____

STREET_____

CITY_____ STATE & ZIP_____

Please Print

- -

MAKING IT: IN LESS THAN AN HOUR

Schiffer Publishing, Ltd.
Box E, Exton, Pa. 19341

Please send me_____ copies of your cookbook at $8.95 each postage included. I enclose $8.95 per copy, a total of $_____ .
Penna. residents, please add $ .54 tax, for each copy.

NAME_____

STREET_____

CITY_____ STATE & ZIP_____

Please Print

- -

MAKING IT: IN LESS THAN AN HOUR

Schiffer Publishing, Ltd.
Box E, Exton, Pa. 19341

Please send me_____ copies of your cookbook at $8.95 each postage included. I enclose $8.95 per copy, a total of $_____ .
Penna. residents, please add $ .54 tax, for each copy.

NAME_____

STREET_____

CITY_____ STATE & ZIP_____

Please Print

MAKING IT: IN LESS THAN AN HOUR

Schiffer Publishing, Ltd.
Box E, Exton, Pa. 19341

     Please send me_____ copies of your cookbook at $8.95 each postage included. I enclose $8.95 per copy, a total of $_____ . Penna. residents, please add $ .54 tax, for each copy.

NAME_____

STREET_____

CITY_____ STATE & ZIP_____

Please Print

MAKING IT: IN LESS THAN AN HOUR

Schiffer Publishing, Ltd.
Box E, Exton, Pa. 19341

     Please send me_____ copies of your cookbook at $8.95 each postage included. I enclose $8.95 per copy, a total of $_____ . Penna. residents, please add $ .54 tax, for each copy.

NAME_____

STREET_____

CITY_____ STATE & ZIP_____

Please Print

MAKING IT: IN LESS THAN AN HOUR

Schiffer Publishing, Ltd.
Box E, Exton, Pa. 19341

     Please send me_____ copies of your cookbook at $8.95 each postage included. I enclose $8.95 per copy, a total of $_____ . Penna. residents, please add $ .54 tax, for each copy.

NAME_____

STREET_____

CITY_____ STATE & ZIP_____

Please Print